Everything
We Do
Matters

Venerable

Wuling

Venerable Wuling is an American Buddhist nun of the Pure Land school of Mahayana Buddhism. More of her writing is available on her blog at www.abuddhistperspective.org

Amitabha Publications, Chicago, 60532
© 2007 by Amitabha Publications
Some rights reserved

12 11 10 09   1 2 3 4 5

ISBN: 978-1-59975-358-4

Library of Congress Control Number: 2007907519

Amida Society

5918 Cloverly Ave, Temple City, CA 91780 U.S.A.
Tel: (1)626-286-5700, (1)626-282-3700
Fax: (1)626-286-7988
Web: www.amtb-la.org
E-mail:amida@amtb-la.org
Printed in Taiwan

In Appreciation

To my mother,
Evelyn Bolender.
I came to visit her for three months but had
the good fortune to be with her for three years
until her passing.
Much of this book was written in her home.

Some lifetimes we are truly blessed
with laughter as well as love.

Contents

EVERYTHING WE DO MATTERS

In a land and time very distant from us, two men encountered one another. One was a Brahmin, a Hindu priest. He realized that the man he was looking at was no ordinary being and so he inquired: "Are you a god?" "No, Brahmin." "Are you an angel?" "No, Brahmin." "Are you a spirit?" "No, Brahmin." "What are you then?" "I am awake," replied the Buddha.

By his own assertion, the Buddha was not a god. He was an ordinary man living in a world engulfed in greed, anger, ignorance, and delusion.

Twenty-five hundred years ago, when the Buddha was teaching what he had awoken to, his world was similar in many ways to our world today. There were great centers of culture, and there were lands of stagnation. There were rulers with great power who thirsted for even more, and there were oppressed people who only wanted to live in peace. There were men who said that they alone held the key to spiritual secrets, and there were those who searched for different answers. There were people who had great wealth, and there were those who had nothing. There were people who said we must change, and there were those who denied there was anything wrong. Perhaps that distant land and time is not that distant after all. Greed, anger, ignorance, and delusion are still very much with us.

In the world today, we hear so much about conflict: Economic conflict between the developed countries and third-world countries. Cultural conflict between the East and the West. Sectarian conflict in the Middle East. Ethnic conflict in Africa. So much pride and arrogance, so much hatred, so much pain. When even government leaders cannot peacefully resolve the world's problems, what are we supposed to do? How can we, individuals without power or influence, hope to accomplish anything positive in the face of such fury and intolerance?

In our technologically-advanced world, is there anything we can learn from this man who rode away one night leaving behind a life of sensory indulgence, privilege, and power to spend the rest of his life walking barefoot across India and Nepal, sleeping under trees, and begging for his food? Is there anything we can learn from this man who awoke to the truth twenty-five hundred years ago?

If we view Buddhism merely as a religion filled with rituals and go no further, no, we will not benefit. Viewing Buddhism in this way, we may put too much energy into creating the perfect practice space. And we may run the risk of becoming engrossed in the accoutrements of practice: robes and meditation cushions, incense and musical instruments. Approaching Buddhism in this way, our time will be spent capturing the appearance of Buddhist practice rather than applying the teachings.

If we view Buddhism solely as a study of morality, concentration, and wisdom, then again, no, we will not benefit. If we merely study Buddhism, we may read many books and gain knowledge, but we will not experience—and we will not savor—the joy of the Dharma. The Dharma is the universal truth that the Buddha himself experienced and then related to us. If we only read about Buddhism, we will have misused our time by intellectualizing the teachings instead of practicing them. Just studying Buddhism, or any faith tradition or ethical teaching, will do nothing to solve our problems. We need to act. But how?

If we concurrently view Buddhism as a teaching of morality, concentration, and wisdom, and we practice it, yes, then—and only then—can Buddhism truly help us. Only when we experience what the Buddha was talking about will we begin to benefit ourselves and our world.

Where do we start? We can start with two fundamental precepts from the Buddha: to do no harm and to purify our minds. He did not tell us to instruct others to correct their faults. He did not say we should force others into thinking as we do or belittle others to make ourselves look superior or wiser. He told us that if we wish to awaken, we would need to stop blaming others for our problems, to stop arguing with others, and to stop judging others.

Instead, we need to look at ourselves, understand our situations, and assume full responsibility for what happens to us. We reap what we sow. Our lives today are the result of what we thought, said, and did in the past. What we think, say, and do today will, likewise, shape our future. If we harm others, we will be harmed. If we love others, we will be loved. If we have peaceful thoughts, we will have peace. Every-thing will come back to us full circle. Thus, everything we do matters.

The Buddha told us not to harm others. How do we accomplish this? Morality—do to others as you would have them do to you. The Buddha expressed the same idea when he said, "Do not hurt others with that which hurts yourself." Mohammed said, "None of you is a believer until you love for your neighbor what you love for yourself." Hillel said, "What is hateful to you, do not do to others." Confucius said, "What you do not wish for yourself, do not do to others." If you would not want someone to lie to you, do not lie to others. If you would be unhappy if someone took something from you, then do not take anything without the owner's permission. If you would be upset if someone spoke harshly to you, then do not speak harshly to others.

The reality is that there is little we can do to quickly and easily bring about change on a global scale. But there is a great deal that each of us can do—and must do—to change ourselves. The only way to achieve world peace is to create peace within each of us. If there are fires to the north, south, east, and west of us, do not expect to avoid getting burned. A person surrounded by fire will suffer. If we want a harmonious society, we must create harmony in our family, in our workplace, and in our communities. Instead of being consumed by the fire of our craving and anger, we need to create peace.

When we hear such words, we are moved, and we nod our heads in agreement. Treating others as we want to be treated sounds wonderful. These truthful words fall like raindrops on hearts that are thirsting for gentleness and serenity. They fill us with joy.

But the minute we stop focusing on the words, we forget! So quickly the awareness and joy fade as we are pulled back into everyday concerns. Perhaps this will happen even as we drive home today. How easy it will be to slip back into selfishness and forget to treat the other person on the road as we wish to be treated. How readily we will make a thoughtless remark about someone and inadvertently pollute our mind and the minds of those with us. Forgetting that we do not want others injecting their harsh words into our peaceful thoughts, we will carelessly intrude on the peaceful thoughts of others.

To practice not harming others, we need concentration—the ability to focus on our chosen task. To not harm others, and thus not harm ourselves, we need to focus on what we are thinking and on what we are about to do. But we rarely do either mindfully.

There are far too many distractions around us. There is so much we want to learn, so many toys we want to possess, so many experiences we want to have—we want, we want, we want. Our desires pull us first in one direction and then almost immediately in another. What we wanted so urgently last year, we want to replace this year. We are pulled by our cravings, so we remain prisoners of our own attachments and aversions—little wonder we cannot concentrate! But learn to concentrate we must. Unless we learn to be masters of our minds, we will continue to be slaves to our emotions.

Do not harm any living being. The Buddha showed us how. Once we begin to rein ourselves in by living morally, we will commit fewer wrongdoings. In this way, we will be less plagued by guilt. We will react less from emotions and more from reason. Harming others less will result in our worrying less. By not wasting time worrying, our minds will be more at ease, and we will be better able to focus on what we wish to: perhaps on our spiritual practice or simply on what we are doing.

As we progressively become calmer, our concentration will enable us to touch our innate wisdom. This is the wisdom that the Buddha experienced and then spoke of. It already lies deep within each of us. But we have yet to enter, much less function from, this clear, intuitive wisdom.

As caring members of society, it is our responsibility to practice the virtues of harmlessness, compassion, and equanimity. These virtues lie deep within us, within our true nature. This true nature is the same as that of all Buddhas. The true nature of Buddhas—their very essence—is loving-kindness, altruism, and tranquility. These qualities lie at the core of their being, and ours.

Although such virtues are already within each one of us, all too often they lie dormant. Why? Because we are thoroughly engrossed in foolish attempts to satisfy our personal desires. We are convinced that our way of doing things is correct and that our happiness lies in possessions and power. Consequently, we are intent on getting others to do things our way and on accumulating wealth and influence. Although we have the same true nature as a Buddha, we fail to experience the wonders of this true nature. We consistently fall back into our bad habits. Thus, we end up acting from our human nature, all the while burying our true nature even deeper within us.

The Buddha knew the problems of humanity for he had experienced them. But he overcame those problems. He awoke through the practice of morality, concentration, and wisdom. He experienced the truth of the cosmos. He found the path to awakening and left clear guidelines to enable us to follow after him. But that was all he could do—leave guidelines.

As compassionate as Buddhas are, they are unable to go against the natural laws of the universe. They know the truth. And they know that the natural laws which govern the universe cannot be changed, not even by a Buddha. So, as much as they want to help us, Buddhas cannot undo what we have already set into motion.

I created my life. Only I can change it. You created your own life. Only you can change it. Others created their lives. Only they can change their lives. Our lives today are the direct result of what we thought, what we said, and what we did in our yesterdays. As we have learned, our todays, just like our yesterdays, are lived in this selfsame world, a world engulfed in greed and anger, a world enveloped in ignorance and delusion.

Greed is our endless craving, and anger is what arises when our greed is unfulfilled. Ignorance is our lack of understanding the truths that underlie what is happening to us and around us. Delusion is mistaking wrong ideas for the truth. Due to our ignorance and delusion, we believe in ideas that are wrong and reject those that are correct and beneficial. But we do so not because we are bad people. Lazy? Yes. Easily distracted? Yes. Impatient and judgmental? Yes. But because we are bad people? No.

Lacking the ability to clearly discern right from wrong, we automatically react out of our bad habits and, consequently, we are impatient and inconsiderate. In most instances, our intentions are not to harm others. We are just so easily caught up in our desires, wishes, and expectations. When these are unfulfilled, in our impatience and disappointment, we give in to anger, which rises from within us, uninvited and unnoticed. So easily, so automatically, we feel resentment and irritation, if not outright rage.

In the grip of these negative feelings, we react to other people, to our situations, not out of the wish to help others but from the compelling urge to protect ourselves. Anger arises when we are selfish, when we are only thinking of what we want but failed to obtain. The other person does not go along with our ideas—we do not receive their agreement and praise for our cleverness. The item we want eludes us—we do not possess the object we are convinced would make us happy. The person we desire rejects us—we are alone and afraid.

All these fears lie at the core of our anger. We convince ourselves that the ideas, the possessions, the person will make us happy. We want it to happen—we expect it to happen! But our expectations fail to materialize. Happiness once again eludes us. Instead of looking at ourselves to see if we perhaps were the cause, we blame others for arguing with us, for not giving us what we deserve to have, for not loving us as we hope. And so our fear of not being admired by others, our fear of not having what others have, our fear of being lonely and alone arise. We strike back defensively at those around us. We strike at those we perceive as having robbed us of what we wanted, of what we felt we deserved to obtain, and of what we believe others already have. We are afraid.

In our fear, we feel vulnerable. In our insecurity and anxiety, our fear gives birth to anger. We may hold our bitterness, resentment, or pain inside, or we may react by striking out at the other person. Either way, we give in to anger once again. In the same way, our family members give in to anger. Friends and co-workers give in to anger. Those with power and the means to inflict great harm give in to anger. And our world is engulfed in greed and disappointment, in ignorance and delusion, and in anger and retaliation.

Not just individuals but groups of people, bound together by ethnicity, religion, or by politics, react in the same way: with greed, fear, anger, retaliation. What is the answer? How do we resolve conflict and attain peace?

Wishful thinking will not end the hatred and intolerance in the world. Merely reading books will not solve our problems. Relying on others certainly does not work. The only way to create peace is through hard work and dedication, and by understanding how much is at stake here. We, each one of us, must be dedicated. We must do the hard work.

But we need not discover how to do the work. The Buddhas have already taught us everything we need to know and shown us the path we need to follow. We can take comfort in the knowledge that although Buddhas cannot get us out of the chaos we have created, they will help us as long as we need them to. This they do by continuing to teach us and showing us the way. We just need to listen and follow their guidance.

Do not harm others. Purify your mind. Do to others as you would have them do to you. Morality, concentration, and wisdom—these provide a proven path to follow. The Buddha reached the end of it twenty-five hundred years ago and awakened. We too can reach the end of the path and awaken. All we need to do is step onto it and, then, let nothing deter us from finding the way to understanding and peace.

MAINTAINING THE CALM, CLEAR MIND

One time when the Buddha was staying in Sravasti, an incident came to his attention. Close to where he was visiting resided a number of monks and nuns. It happened that when some nuns were spoken ill of, one of the monks would become angry. When that monk was spoken ill of, the nuns would become angry. After confirming with the monk that this was accurate, the Buddha advised the monk that he should discipline himself and hold the thoughts: "My mind will not change [be swayed], I will not utter evil words, I will abide with compassion and loving kindness without an angry thought."[1]

---

[1] Sister Upalavanna, translator, *Kakacupama Sutta,* MN 21, (http://www.saigon.com/~anson/ebud/majjhima/021-kakacupama-sutta-e1.htm)

The Buddha then told the monastics to always remember that even ordinarily calm minds can be disturbed in difficult times. So the monastics needed to train themselves to remain calm, regardless of the situation. The Buddha recounted how there was once a woman who lived in the same city where he and the monastics currently were. Everyone regarded the woman as gentle and quiet. She had a slave named Kali who was clever and hardworking. Kali wondered whether her mistress was as mild-tempered as she seemed. Might her mistress actually be hiding a bad temper? Perhaps Kali was so efficient that her mistress had not had cause to reveal her true temper!

Kali decided to test her mistress by getting up later than usual one morning. When the mistress saw Kali and asked her why she got up late, Kali responded that she did not have a reason. The mistress became angry. The next morning Kali got up even later. Once more, her mistress questioned her. And once more, Kali replied that she did not have a reason. When this happened yet again on the third morning, the infuriated mistress struck Kali. Bleeding, Kali ran out of the house crying out that her

mistress had hit her because she had gotten up late!
Word of what had happened spread and with it the
report that the mistress was actually violent and bad-
tempered.

The Buddha pointed out to the monastics that as
long as they did not hear anything disagreeable or
unpleasant, most of them were quiet and well behaved. But when they heard something
objectionable, such words became a test as to
whether they were truly calm and polite. The Buddha gave an example: Monks may be gentle and kind
because they have everything they need. But if they
become upset when their needs go unfulfilled, then
they are not truly gentle.

The Buddha explained to the monks that there are
five aspects of speech by which others may speak to
them: "timely or untimely, true or false, affectionate
or harsh, beneficial or unbeneficial, with a mind of
good-will or with inner hate."[2] In these circumstances, they should train themselves by thinking:
"Our minds will be unaffected and we will say no evil

---

[2] Thanissaro Bhikkhu, *Kalama Sutta*, AN III.65 (1994)
(http://accesstoinsight.org/canon/sutta/anguttara/an03-
065.html)

words. We will remain sympathetic to that person's welfare, with a mind of good will and with no inner hate. We will keep pervading him with an awareness imbued with good will and, beginning with him, we will keep pervading the all-encompassing world with an awareness imbued with good will—abundant, expansive, immeasurable, free from hostility, free from ill will."[3]

The Buddha continued that even if robbers were to carve the monks up limb by limb, with a two-handed saw, the monk who became angry even at that would not be doing the Buddha's bidding. He instructed the monastics that even under such circumstances, they needed to train themselves to maintain an unaffected mind and to continuously pervade the universe with thoughts of goodwill, by eliminating hatred and not speaking evil words.

The Buddha asked if there would be any speech they could not endure were they to follow this guidance. They responded that there was none. He then told them that they should call to mind often the Simile of the Saw, for doing so would bring them

---

[3] Ibid.

happiness and great benefit.

The Buddha was teaching them to discipline themselves and to train by remembering these words of advice whenever they heard people speaking to them using speech that was timely or untimely, true or false, affectionate or harsh, beneficial or unbeneficial, with a mind of good-will or with inner hate. In other words, they were to train themselves by remembering these words of advice at all times.

First, the monks were to train so that their minds remained unaffected. To maintain a calm, clear, and unperturbed mind, we should not allow that which we see, hear, taste, touch, or think to disturb and thus taint our pure mind. Whatever has been perceived must not move the mind but be allowed to fall away, just as an image moving in front of a mirror is reflected but is no longer present after passing out of sight.

Also, the monks were to say no evil words. Like them, we can endeavor to never again say words that are false, harsh, divisive, or enticing. This guideline of saying only what is correct, honest, and beneficial enables us to keep our speech proper. So often when we are speaking with others, we do not say anything helpful but instead indulge in idle chatter or frivolous talk. If there is nothing correct, honest, and beneficial to say, it would be wiser to remain quiet. This way we will not have to regret what we have said or wonder how to undo the harm we have done.

When speaking with others, it is also important to find the right time to discuss sensitive matters. Embarrassing or hurting someone because we chose the wrong time to speak to them will cause additional suffering. Furthermore, it will do nothing to correct the situation. We need to find both the right words and the right time to say those words.

Next, the monks were to remain sympathetic to that person's welfare, with a mind of good will and without hate. We need compassion not just for the abused but also for the one who is the abuser. One who hurts others does not understand causality, does not understand that by doing this he or she will continue to be pulled back again and again into the cycle of inflicting and receiving pain. People who hurt others do not understand that the persons they are hurting had hurt them in the past. By retaliating now, they are just perpetuating this cycle of pain.

We need sympathy and compassion to understand

how both the victimizer and the victim are caught in this cycle. Unaware of the cause and effect that has brought them to this point; they are unable to act wisely. This is certainly understandable. How many of us have learned about causality? We should understand what is really happening when negative things occur in our lives. But when such things happen, how often are we able to remain calm and react wisely?

If we are sympathetic to others' welfare while maintaining goodwill, commiseration, and loving-kindness for all people, then we will not judge others. We will not say that this person is right and that person is wrong because we will come to understand that we do not know what is really happening, that we will likely mistake falsity for truth. But if we are able to regard both friend and foe with sympathy and loving-kindness, we will then be able to practice the nonjudgmental, unconditional giving of love and thus wish for all beings to be happy.

Next, the monks were to have a mind without hatred. Not talking harshly to others, not being sarcastic, and not lashing out blindly are ways to control anger. But we need to go further. Ideally, we should not even hold anger in our hearts. Holding on to our anger will taint everything we do: when we interact with others from a mind of bitterness and frustration, we will inflict our anger on others.

In conclusion, the Buddha told the monks that they were to keep permeating the person who spoke to them out of ill will with an awareness imbued with good will. Beginning with that person, they were to keep pervading the all-encompassing world with an awareness imbued with good will—abundant, expansive, immeasurable, free from hostility, and free from ill will. Initially, we can start this training with those who are close to us: family and friends who care for us. We start here because it is easier for us to love those who love us and who are kind to us. It is much more difficult to love those whom we have negative feelings for.

Once we establish this mind of compassion and goodwill for family and friends, we can then begin to expand it to include people we casually encounter, people whom we have no strong positive or negative feelings for. Accomplishing this, we can broaden this mind of benevolence to include people we dislike, and eventually even those we hate. If we can keep widening this mind, we will gradually be able to accommodate many others in an ever-widening circle. Then, we can open up this caring mind to include all beings throughout the universe. The more encompassing this caring mind is, the greater our respect for all beings and all things will be. Our regard for others will bring us tranquility because we will not fall back into anger, frustration, and resentment.

The Buddha spoke of the Simile of the Saw to show us that even when something horrible happens, we should not feel aversion toward the one who is hurting another. If we react to an abusive or violent situation with animosity, then we are making the situation worse. We will have allowed another's anger to destroy our peace of mind and rob us of our mind of compassion.

If we fall into the habit of proceeding from bitterness and anger, then we will be reacting out of blind, destructive emotion. When we do this, we are not helping anyone—not the other person, not ourselves—because we will become emotionally ensnared in the other person's situation. If we can remain calm, we will have a much better chance of successfully utilizing our innate wisdom and thus knowing how to be truly helpful.

Reacting to violence with violence only increases the existing hostility. It may appear to solve the problem at that moment but we are actually planting seeds for more antagonism in the future. If only we had been able to act with wisdom in the past, then we would already have resolved this enmity. But having failed to do so once, we have enabled it to grow. And if we do not resolve it with understanding today, this anger and violence will increase and be even worse the next time it erupts. As the Buddha said, hatred never ceases by hatred but by the absence of hatred.

Often when I speak of this to people, they would ask about a situation where they see someone hurting another person or even attacking someone we love. How does one react in such an emotional situation?

This is exactly when we need to have a calm mind. If we become angry, then we will just charge blindly into the situation and might even begin to behave violently ourselves. With a calm mind, we will have the wisdom to know what to do even in dangerous circumstances.

The sutras have accounts in which the Buddha encountered angry people and violent situations. But he knew the right words to get through to the people to help them stop what they were doing. We do not know the right words because our minds are not calm enough. Only when our minds are tranquil and clear will we be able to access our innate, nonjudgmental wisdom so that we will know the right words to speak and the right actions to take.

Ideally, when we see someone hurting another or when someone is trying to harm us, we need to understand that this is a karmic consequence of something that happened in the past. With this understanding of causality and with the understanding that this body is not "I," we would not fight back in emotionally-charged moments when attacked by another. In the *Diamond Sutra*, we read of a bodhisattva who was viciously attacked and killed while he was meditating quietly on a mountain. But due to his level of understanding and his calm, clear mind, he felt no anger, no hatred.

I think it is safe to say that we are not yet at that level. Unable to react as awakened beings, we can defend the person being attacked or ourselves or alternatively try to escape without hurting the one who is being violent. We should try to do everything possible not to make the situation worse. The more we practice meditative concentration, the easier it would be to react from our calm mind. We will then know how to react wisely in all situations.

But the situation that we are talking about is a hypothetical one that most likely would never happen. A much more probable situation would be one where someone cuts us off as we are driving down the road. This happens all the time. Instead of acting out of anger by blowing the horn or trying to speed up to cut the other person off, how might we react?

Recently, a young woman told me that she practices patience while driving. She allows herself ample time to arrive at her destination. This enables her to drive at a moderate speed. If someone cuts her off, no problem! Not in a rush, she is able to remain unaffected by the carelessness or rudeness of others. She might arrive at her destination a few minutes later than if she had been speeding and weaving in and out of traffic, but it is worth it because she arrives in a calm, happy mood.

These are the situations we encounter—life's daily annoyances and frustrations. Whether it be the rudeness of the clerk in a store, the telemarketer we cannot get rid of, or the person at work who always argues with us, these are the real-life circumstances that we encounter countless times during the day. These are the very times when we should practice what the Buddha spoke of.

If in small everyday situations we can start responding from the mind that is not swayed by emotions—the mind of sympathy and love that is free of hatred and bitterness—we will be planting good seeds. These good seeds will mature into good conditions. With good conditions, we can continue to practice. Our practice of morality and of respecting and not harming others will further increase our good conditions. With such conditions, the bad seeds will not have the opportunity to mature, and we will not find ourselves in violent situations.

Following the Buddha's advice, we should strive to never lose our calm, clear mind and never utter harsh or evil words but instead treat others with a mind of sympathy and compassion. Letting go of our anger, we will permeate the entire world with an awareness imbued with concern—unreserved, infinite, and free from hostility and ill will.

Encountering situations that are potentially upsetting and that could make us angry, we should not give in to our destructive emotions. Our habitual recourse to that anger has resulted in the quarrels, fights, and wars that are engulfing our world today. Instead of mindlessly cultivating anger, recall the Simile of the Saw.

If we can keep training our minds to be serene and to empathize with others, we will gradually uncover our wisdom and know how to be of help to others in any situation. Remember that upholding a calm, clear mind is usually easier to accomplish when we are not emotionally involved and when we do not have anything at stake. As we accomplish this in minor, everyday events, we will see that it works. This will give us the confidence to apply this same teaching in more trying situations. As with everything worthwhile, this will take time and require a lot of patience. But with time, we will gradually develop this mind of serenity, commiseration, and compassion.

VENGEANCE

We read in the sutras how, one year, a conflict arose
between two monks. It was a relatively small event
that triggered the animosity but it gradually split
them and their fellow monks into two main groups. A
smaller third group watched what was happening but
did not take sides. Members of each main group
were convinced that they were right and that the
other group was wrong. As the situation worsened,
the two groups even began to practice separately.

Growing increasingly concerned with the group
conflict, some of the monks who did not take sides
went to the Buddha and told him what was happening. He spoke to both groups and encouraged them
to resume practicing harmoniously, to not be attached to their own viewpoints, and to try to
understand those of others. But the situation continued to deteriorate.

The Buddha was again asked to please try to reconcile the two opposing groups of monks. He went to the monastery and for a second time spoke of the need for peace and unity within the Buddhist community. One monk stood up and requested the Buddha to please return to his meditation, saying that they would resolve the situation themselves. Once more, the Buddha asked the monks to stop fighting and to return to harmony. The same monk repeated what he had said and, in so doing, rejected the Buddha's guidance.

The Buddha then told the monks about a series of events that took place long ago. King Brahmadata ruled a large kingdom and commanded a strong army. King Dighiti, who ruled a smaller kingdom, heard that Brahmadata was about to invade his kingdom. Knowing he could never defeat Brahmadata's army and that many of his soldiers would lose their lives in a futile battle, King Dighiti felt it would be best if he and his queen fled. So they went into hiding in another city. A short time later, the queen gave birth to Prince Dighavu. When the prince was older, King Dighiti began to fear what would happen if King Brahmadata found all three of them. As a result, arrangements were made for the prince to live elsewhere.

One day, the king and queen were recognized, captured, and taken to be executed. By chance, Prince Dighavu was on his way to see his parents, whom he had not seen in a long time. He was about to rush to them when his father cried out, "Don't, my dear Dighavu, be far-sighted. Don't be near-sighted. For vengeance is not settled through vengeance. Vengeance is settled through non-vengeance."[4] The King repeated his warning two more times, adding that he was not deranged, and said that those with heart would understand what he meant.

None of the villagers knew who Dighavu was or what the king was talking about. Heeding his father's warning, Dighavu managed to restrain himself. He watched his parents being executed and dismembered. That night he bought wine and gave it to the guards, who soon became drunk. He then made a pyre, gathered his parent's remains, placed them on the pyre, and set fire to it. After paying his final respects to his parents, he went into the forest to

---

[4] Ibid.

mourn their death.

A while later, after coming out of hiding, Dighavu managed to obtain a job as an apprentice at an elephant stable next to the palace. One day, when King Brahmadata heard Dighavu singing and playing the lute, he was moved by the sound and arranged for Dighavu to work in his palace. Serving the king and always acting to please him, Dighavu gradually won the king's trust.

One day, while King Brahmadata was out hunting, Dighavu, who was driving the king's chariot, deliberately drove the chariot away from the rest of the hunting party. Not long after, the king said he wished to take a nap and soon went to sleep, using Dighavu's lap for a pillow. Dighavu's moment of revenge had come. He took out his sword, but suddenly his father's words came back to him and he put the sword away. A second time, he drew and then sheathed his sword.

After Dighavu drew his sword for the third time, his father's words—simple and gentle—hit home. They touched Dighavu's heart that was full of hatred and consumed by a desire for vengeance. His heart knew the truth of his father's words and understood

their import. Heeding his father's words, Dighavu
awakened at last to the compassion and wisdom
extant in that selfsame heart. He was able to put not
only his sword down but his hatred and his desire for
vengeance as well.

Suddenly, the king awoke in great alarm. He told
Dighavu that he dreamed that Prince Dighavu was
about to kill him! Instinctively, Dighavu drew his
sword yet again and announced that he was Prince
Dighavu. The king immediately begged Dighavu not
to kill him. With his compassion and wisdom overcoming his hatred and desire for vengeance, Dighavu
was able to put away his sword. Then, in turn, he
begged for the king's forgiveness. The king and the
prince spared each other's life, and each vowed never
to harm the other. They then returned to the castle.

Back at the palace, the king asked his ministers
what they would do if they could find Prince
Dighavu. After hearing their brutal descriptions of
what they would do, the king told them what had
just transpired. He then turned to Dighavu and
asked the meaning of his father's last words.

Dighavu explained that *do not be far-sighted*
meant one should not hold on to a wish for retalia-

tion. *Do not be near-sighted* meant one should not readily break one's friendship with another. Additionally, *vengeance is not settled through vengeance.* *Vengeance is settled through non-vengeance* enabled Dighavu to realize that if he sought revenge for the deaths of his parents by killing the king, the king's supporters would retaliate by killing him. Then Dighavu's supporters would in turn kill the king's supporters. This is why vengeance never ends through vengeance. In sparing each other's lives, both the king and the prince ended vengeance by letting go of it.

Dighavu's father's words to Dighavu to not be far-sighted meant not to hold on to the wish for vengeance. In the previous talk, we learned how the Buddha had told the monastics on several occasions that they should always train themselves as follows: "Our minds will be unaffected and we will say no evil words. We will remain sympathetic to that person's welfare, with a mind of good will, and with no inner hate. We will keep pervading him with an awareness imbued with good will and, beginning with him, we will keep pervading the all-encompassing world with an awareness imbued with good will—abundant, expansive, immeasurable, free from hostility, free from ill will."[5] If we give in to anger, our mind will be shaken and be moved from its naturally clear, tranquil state. If we hold on to our wish for vengeance, we will harbor evil words as well as a mind of hatred and bitterness. Then this mind will have no room for empathy or good will.

If anyone had a right to feel hatred and fear, surely it was King Dighiti. Yet, when confronted with a truly terrifying situation, his overriding thought was to protect his son. He did not cry out for his son to save him and his queen, or for Dighavu to save his own life by fleeing, but instead spoke to his son's heart and told him not to come forward. He then warned Dighavu not to hold on to resentment, not to readily destroy a friendship, and not to seek revenge. The king had the presence of mind to know in an instant just the precise words that would strike the right chord in the heart of his son, even when he had not seen him for some years.

Imagine the level of restraint required to be able to speak wisely out of love and empathy instead of

---

[5] Ibid.

anger and terror. Imagine, with eminent danger all around, how focused the mind had to be. Imagine the dignity it took to remain calm. How many of us today have even a fraction of such restraint and dignity? How much do we practice restraint in our daily lives? And how often? How dignified are we in our demeanor and behavior?

Picture in your mind an image of the Buddha—an awakened being. What qualities does this image bring to mind? Restraint and dignity. Patience and compassion. Contentment and great ease. These are the qualities we need to uncover within ourselves if we are to, like him, awaken.

But our lives today are so frantic. We have so much to do. We rush from one task to another. With so much to do, we must be important people! It is so easy to be seduced by current ideas of what a successful person is. We have seriously strayed from our inner virtues. We practice little restraint. We exhibit little dignity. We are hurting ourselves. And even worse, we are causing great harm to our children. We are setting them on a path that will lead them even farther away from their innate goodness and virtues.

Instead of passing on our bad habits of self-indulgence and instant gratification to our children, we need to teach them what is important in life— how to become truly contented and caring people. Contented, caring people have no room for craving or hatred in their hearts. Such people have no room for thoughts of retaliation in their minds. Such people are worthy of the respect and trust of others. Such people are at ease with life. And when sad or even terrible things happen, they are not overcome by fear or sorrow. They are able to control their fear and transform it into love. They know the futility of doing otherwise; they know the great harm they can do to those they love more than life itself.

Contented and caring people are able to consider not what they themselves want but what others need. Placing those needs above personal desires, such virtuous people are able to think and react with restraint and dignity. They are able to give wisely to others what will truly benefit others.

In the account of Dighavu, his father, the king, gave his son two wonderful gifts: insight and life itself. Through his words and his actions, with dignity and restraint, he was able to send his son a powerful message that enabled him to overcome the desire for revenge. The king taught Dighavu that one should not hold on to but should, instead, let go of anger and bitterness.

Fortunately, most of us do not face such horrific moments. Yes, we have arguments with family members and friends, and we often find ourselves having to interact with people we do not like. But as disagreeable as these occurrences are, they are certainly not life threatening. And yet when we encounter frustrating or trying situations, how many of us are able to remain calm or to respond from wisdom? How many of us would, instead, complain to all who would listen or grumble to ourselves? How often have our minds been shaken from their clear, tranquil states? How often do we use evil words that are harsh or false? How often do we hold on to our anger privately and then nurture that anger with our thoughts?

As Dighavu's father said, do not hold on to the wish for revenge. We can choose to wrap ourselves in our resentment and bitterness and, in so doing, reject peace and happiness—the results of this type of reaction can be viewed daily on the evening news. Or, we can choose to broaden the scope of our compassion and wish for an end to the suffering of all beings. We can choose to create peace within ourselves, and in this way bring peace to others.

Next, in the account the Buddha related, the king told his son to not be near-sighted, which meant to not readily break a friendship. The about-to-be-executed king wanted his son to understand the value of friendship and trust. To befriend others, we need to have trust in people and be trustworthy ourselves. Realizing that Dighavu was about to kill him, King Brahmadata knelt down and begged Dighavu to spare his life. We could say that since Dighavu was about to kill the king, this was not an act of trust but one of fear and desperation.

But then Dighavu remembered his father's advice for him to not readily break a friendship. Suddenly aware of the meaning of these words, Dighavu put away his sword. Then, he asked for the king's forgiveness. This was an act of great trust on his part. He compounded this trust by returning to the king's palace, thereby putting his own life at even greater risk. This time the king returned the prince's trust by telling his ministers what had happened and handing back the conquered kingdom to Dighavu. To further deepen the bond between them, he gave Dighavu his daughter in marriage.

In our trust, we need to be sincere. It was the prince's sincerity that so moved the king. Too often, when we do something, we do so with hesitation and doubt. This doubt may well prevent us from doing what we know to be right. Or our motives for doing something may well be selfish. Dighavu's were not. He wanted to honor his father's words and not carry hatred and bitterness in his heart. His wish to do so was so strong that he was willing to sacrifice his own life to let go of hatred and vengeance. This was not easy for him to do. He struggled with himself, pulling out his sword three times to kill the sleeping king. But in his heart, he knew the truth of his father's words, and in the end, he was able to lay aside his wish for revenge.

So often, we act out of self-interest, unwilling even to sacrifice our pride, much less our lives. In our struggle with our conscience, we also have doubts and, like Dighavu, we also hesitate. Thoughts that we are right and that we know what will make us happy and bring us what we desire keep bubbling up from inside us. Unlike Dighavu, in really important matters, we repeatedly fall short of acting on what we sense to be right. We do so not because we are bad people. We do so because we are careless and because we have gotten into the habit of giving ourselves excuses to not do what is right. We tell ourselves we deserve to feel the way we do. So, with hesitation and doubt, we may not do what we know we should. And even if we do what we know to be right, the hesitation is still there. Moreover, this hesitation will be apparent to others around us.

But if we can completely overcome the negative, selfish inclination and wholeheartedly do what we know to be right, our sincerity will shine through. If we are sincere—truly sincere—we will touch others. And if we trust others with such palpable sincerity that they are able to feel it, then we ourselves will be deemed trustworthy and honorable.

Dighavu's father's last words to him were that vengeance was not settled through vengeance but through non-vengeance. Seeking revenge never ends hatred but, instead, causes it to grow. Dighavu explained that if he had sought revenge by killing the king, the king's supporters would in turn seek revenge by killing him. Then his own supporters would retaliate by the killing those of the king. And on and on and on this cycle of killing would continue. If, however, the prince and the king spared each other's lives, the hatred would end then and there. And so when that happened, then and there the hatred died out.

Hatred is a fire that if left unchecked will consume all those it touches. Adding fuel to a fire only increases it. Not supplying the fuel will cause the fire to burn itself out. If we keep fueling the fire of anger and hatred with thoughts of self-justification and self-benefit, of bitterness and resentment, we will never let go of our anger. Eventually, it will consume and destroy us all, for those who are surrounded by fire will inevitably be burned.

Dighavu's father had enabled his love and concern for his son to overcome any anger or hatred he might have felt for King Brahmadata or his soldiers. Dighavu, too, was able to let go of his hatred for a conqueror who had ordered the murder and dismemberment of Dighavu's parents while he looked on helplessly. We, on the other hand, have great difficulty letting go of anger caused by those who keep us from doing what we wish to do, who inconvenience us, or who simply annoy us. We hold on to the slights of others and dream of showing them how clever we are at retaliating.

"Don't, my dear Dighavu, be far-sighted. Don't be near-sighted. For vengeance is not settled through vengeance. Vengeance is settled through non-vengeance." Do not wish for revenge. Be trustworthy, and do not readily break a friendship. End hatred and find peace by letting go of pain and bitterness.

These few words spoken by Dighavu's father, despite their simplicity and gentleness, succeeded in touching a heart that had been overcome with sorrow and consumed with hatred, causing it to let go of the desire for vengeance and thereby awakening the compassion and wisdom extant in that selfsame heart. This very wisdom and compassion was precisely what Dighavu awakened to.

As the Buddha said, we should train ourselves so that our minds remain unaffected by pleasant or adverse conditions and our speech is always benevolent. Our minds should be without hatred as we pervade the universe with goodwill that is abundant, unreserved, and endless.

THE POISONS OF GREED, ANGER, AND IGNORANCE

Once when the Buddha was at the Jeta Grove Monastery, he asked the monastics how they would explain the three poisons of greed, anger, and ignorance to monks who followed other teachings. The monastics replied that they wished to explain to others as the Buddha would, so would he please teach them how to best explain these negative states of mind. He replied that greed arises from thinking of *pleasant* objects and situations in a mistaken way. Once greed has arisen, this thinking of pleasant things will cause it to intensify.

Through our own personal experience, we can see what the Buddha meant. When we see an object or watch others enjoying an activity that we view as pleasant, we want to own the object or to undergo a similar experience. We want to possess a newer model of something we already own. We want to go to the same vacation spot a co-worker visited. We want to indulge ourselves because we feel that we deserve it or perhaps because we want to cheer ourselves up after something disappointing has happened.

And so we want—we crave—things and experiences. But as the Buddha explained, craving leads to suffering, for craving inexorably leads to more craving. Unquenchable, it grows like an addiction. The more we have and the more we experience, the more we want. Our ever-increasing greed results in our lives becoming more stressful as our craving for objects and experiences far surpasses our ability to obtain them. And so we fall deeper and deeper into suffering.

Why does all this happen? It happens because we mistakenly think that pleasant things, be they material objects or experiences, will make us happy. But happiness is a mental state. Happiness is not a quality inherent in material possessions or experiences. Whether or not something makes us happy depends on what we tell ourselves. As Shakespeare wrote in *Hamlet*, "There is nothing either good or bad, but thinking makes it so." That is, it is our thinking that makes us happy or sad. We can tell ourselves that to be happy we need more pleasant objects and situations. Or, we can tell ourselves that wanting more inevitably leads to more wanting and thus to more suffering.

Next, the Buddha explained that anger arises from thinking of *unpleasant* objects and situations in a mistaken way. Once anger arises as the result of such mistaken thinking, it increases.

Again, our personal experiences will bear this out. When we see an object or an occurrence that we view as unpleasant, feelings of resentment, bitterness, and anger can easily arise. We want the experience to stop. We want to be rid of the undesirable object. We want the annoying person to go away. If only these would happen, then we would be happy.

But such thinking, as the Buddha said, is mistaken. Just as the presence of objects and experiences does not necessarily make us happy, neither does their absence. Attempting to satisfy our emotional desires will not lead to happiness. In truth, wanting to stop that which is unpleasant only leads to more wanting, more emotional reactions, more turmoil—not happiness. Not yet realizing this, we continue to buy more tickets to get back on our emotional roller coaster of wanting, attainment, disappointment, and anger.

What should we do instead of falling back into this negative pattern? In a previous talk in this series, we learned of the Buddha urging the monastics to hold the thought "My mind will never be shaken." In other words, our minds should remain stable and focused. We should neither feel attached to pleasant sensations nor feel averse to those that are unpleasant. If we can accomplish this, we will remain content with what we have and calm in any circumstance in which we find ourselves. Content and calm, we will know how to act wisely. Our anger will gradually diminish, and, eventually, cease to arise.

The Buddha concluded by explaining that ignorance arises from wrong thoughts. Once ignorance has arisen, these wrong thoughts will cause ignorance to intensify. Understanding this, one would know how best to view properly both pleasant and unpleasant happenings. If one were able to act from this understanding, then greed and anger should not arise. And even if they did, one would be able to eliminate the greed and overcome the anger. If one looks at life properly, ignorance should not arise. But if it should, one would be able to overcome it.

Here, the Buddha spoke about wrong thoughts. Wrong thoughts are our personal opinions, which arise in response to external sensory stimuli. Relying on this sensory input, we think about what we have encountered and draw conclusions based on what we have seen, heard, smelled, tasted, and touched. Then, we begin to label some things good and others bad, some pleasant and others unpleasant. In other words, we begin to discriminate, seeing duality in everything.

The fundamental flaw in this process is the reliance on our senses. What we fail to consider is the fact that our breadth of exposure is minimal at best and that our senses may well be faulty. Consider the Buddha's account of a group of men blind from birth trying to describe an elephant. Each of the men was taken to a different part of the elephant: its head, an ear, a tusk, its trunk, its stomach, a foot, its tail, and the tuft of its tail. The blind men in turn said that the elephant was like a pot, a basket, a ploughshare, a plow, a storehouse, a pillar, a pestle, and a brush. The men then began to argue with one another and even came to blows over the matter.

These reasonable but limited answers were the result of knowing only a part of the truth, not the whole. And sadly, like those blind men, most of us also encounter only a part of the truth. We, too, cling stubbornly to our own viewpoints, convinced that we have all the facts. And thinking that we have all the facts and feeling confident of our conclusions, we reject the views of others. Thus, our ignorance arises from our wrong thoughts. The manifestation of our ignorance is our attachment to our wrong thoughts, and this inevitably intensifies our ignorance.

On another day, a monk who followed other teachings asked Venerable Ananda what happens to those who gave in to the three poisons. Ananda replied that those who gave in to greed, anger, and ignorance will themselves become victims of those selfsame poisons. Thus, they harm themselves, not just others, and must face the painful outcomes of what they have done. Since greed will lead one to have impure thoughts and to engage in flawed behavior, those who rid themselves of greed do not undergo these painful outcomes.

When our minds are impure, our thoughts arise from greed, anger, and ignorance. They also arise from *arrogance*, our belief that in some way we are superior to others. But the Buddha explained to us that we all have the same true nature. So while our past karmas result in our having lived different lives, and those lives may appear to be better than others, our current lives are only a tiny snapshot of our innumerable lifetimes. In this lifetime, we may be smarter or more privileged than other people. But these roles could be reversed in our next lifetime. Suddenly, those whom we deemed inferior to us will become superior; our arrogance will come back to haunt us. As is said, "Pride goeth before the fall."

Our thoughts may also arise from *doubt*. For example, we may doubt that we have the same true nature as a Buddha, and thus doubt our ability to, like him, awaken. We may doubt that causality functions all around us and within us, throughout all time and space. We may doubt that the mind of the Buddhas and the mind of all beings are all-pervasive—that we are all one. Finally, our thoughts may arise from *delusion*, our belief in erroneous ideas.

Due to all this greed, anger, ignorance, arrogance, doubt, and delusion, our minds are full of wandering and discriminating thoughts. We get caught up in thoughts of liking or disliking, of good or bad, of favorable or unfavorable situations. No longer calm—no longer pure—our minds are constantly affected by our environment.

In this agitated, emotional state, we may or may not act out of good intentions. But even if we act out of our good intentions, they will often backfire because our logic was faulty to begin with. So we end up harming others and ourselves. Mistaking right for wrong and wrong for right, we make bad decisions and must suffer the outcomes our actions have wrought, not because someone judges this to be so, but because causality—cause and effect—is a universal, natural law. Our good intentions may mitigate the outcomes to some degree, but we will still have to undergo what we have brought about through our impure behavior.

When we have overcome our greed, anger, and ignorance, we will not commit such offenses because we will no longer be deluded; we will no longer mistake wrong for right. Our minds will be calm and clear.

Having let go of attachments, arrogance, and selfishness, we will no longer act from discriminations that result from faulty conclusions based on sensory input. Instead, we will act from our inherent wisdom.

Ananda further explained to the monk that those who give in to greed do not understand what is meant by benefiting self, benefiting others, and benefiting all.

Again, we can see from our experience that our craving is usually of a selfish nature: we want something either for ourselves or for those close to us. The satisfaction of this craving is a temporary sense-indulgence that brings us short-lived happiness.

The only way to truly benefit ourselves is to awaken—in other words, to transcend the cycle of rebirth—whereby we obtain lasting liberation and genuine happiness. Until we free ourselves from rebirth, we will not be liberated. As long as we remain within the cycle of rebirth, we are bound by craving and ignorance and will not find true liberation or happiness.

In benefiting others, we move beyond thoughts of self to those of others. At this point, we will realize that all beings, not just ourselves, wish to eliminate suffering and attain happiness. With this realization, we will want to help others accomplish this. We begin by wishing that those we love and care for would attain happiness. Then we wish the same for those we do not know and, gradually, for those we do not like. Ultimately, we will develop the wish for all beings to be free from suffering and to attain happiness.

When we shift the focus of our wish for happiness and liberation away from just ourselves, we will begin to think less of our own happiness. Instead of looking at everything in a self-centered way, we will transform our thoughts into those of caring for others. We will stop asking what is in it for us and will instead ask how we can help others.

The concepts of benefiting ourselves and benefiting others occur at a low level of realization. When our understanding reaches a higher level, we will realize that all beings are one and that there is no duality between self and other. To benefit one being is to benefit all beings. Therefore, to benefit others is to benefit oneself. Realizing this interconnectivity among all beings will enable us to realize that we do not need to worry about self-benefit because when we help the whole, we help ourselves. So, there is no need to worry about "me."

The more we can wholeheartedly aspire to help all beings, the more goodness we will generate. This goodness will in turn create favorable conditions that will enable us to help others even more.

Finally, Ananda cautioned that greed blinds one,

blocks one's wisdom, increases ignorance, and thus obstructs awakening.

It is our craving that causes our suffering—because craving blinds us to reality and disturbs our pure mind. Leaving our calm and clear state, we become embroiled in a cycle of wanting, obtaining, and then wanting even more. The more agitated we become, the less we are able to concentrate, and the deeper we bury our wisdom inside us. Not able to reach our wisdom, we fall prey to ignorance and delusion. We become more afflicted. Our worries increase.

But this does not have to happen. We can be free of greed, anger, and ignorance through moral self-discipline. With moral behavior, our minds will be more settled, and we will be able to achieve meditative concentration. As this meditative concentration enables us to gain more control over our thoughts, and consequently our emotions, we will begin to touch our inherent wisdom. As we continue to act from that inherent wisdom, we will gradually rid ourselves of greed, overcome anger, and uproot our ignorance. Our minds will remain clear and calm in all situations, and we will gradually leave suffering behind and attain lasting liberation and happiness.

GOODWILL, COMPASSION, AND EQUANIMITY

One time, when the Buddha was in Kalama, he spoke to the people there about the three poisons of greed, anger, and ignorance. One who is a student of the Buddhas and who is free of the three poisons will pervade all directions "with an awareness imbued with *good will*: abundant, expansive, immeasurable, free from hostility, free from ill will."[6]

This student will also keep pervading the six directions of north, south, east, west, above, and below—everywhere and in every respect throughout the cosmos—with an awareness imbued with *compassion and equanimity*, both of which are "abundant, expansive, immeasurable, free from hostility, free from ill will."[7]

---

[6] Ibid.
[7] Ibid.

First, the Buddha spoke of goodwill, or loving-kindness, which is feeling and showing concern. It is the wish that all beings be well and secure—that they be happy. With goodwill, we will act purely and without any personal agenda or selfish motives. We will happily forego our personal desires and, instead, focus on the needs of others. Listening carefully to them will enable us to understand what they are feeling and thinking: their wants, their needs, and their aspirations. If we are wrapped up in thoughts of what we, ourselves, have done or wish to do, our thoughts will be of what was or what might be—not of what is. If we are wrapped up in thoughts of self-benefit and ego, our thoughts will be of ourselves, not of other people. So we need to let go of thoughts of self. We need to broaden our minds to focus on others. And to do this, we need a mind and heart of compassion.

Compassion is the intention and capability to lessen suffering and, ultimately, to transform this suffering. When we adopt an awareness imbued with compassion, we seek to ease others' pain. But in our wish to help, more often than not, we react emotionally and end up getting carried away by our feelings.

At times we empathize so completely with what someone is going through that we subject ourselves to the same distress. So instead of one person suffering, there are now two miserable people!

Instead of reacting emotionally, we need to learn to temper our compassion with wisdom. Then we will know how to better help one another. We will also realize that an individual's circumstances are the result of past karmas. Therefore, it may well be next to impossible for us to improve another's situation. This realization does not mean that we should stop caring about others or dismiss their difficulties as being their own fault. It means we understand that our wanting to alleviate their suffering may instead be of benefit to them in the future, in ways we cannot foresee.

So be compassionate, but do not focus on getting immediate positive results. Do not get wrapped up in egoistic thoughts, thinking that "I" can fix the problem. Without such expectations, we will not be disappointed or saddened when our attempts to help end in failure or, worse, aggravate the situation. We will not know how best to help if we fail to temper our compassion with wisdom. In other words, the person we want to help may not have the requisite conditions for us to do so.

When we stop focusing on immediate results and instead focus on just helping others, our compassion will ultimately benefit all beings. By planting the seeds of compassion—the wish for all beings to be happy and free of suffering—we can be confident that we have indeed helped others.

If we feel compassion for only certain people, then our compassion is limited, and thus our ability to lessen suffering in the future will likewise be limited. But when our compassion for all beings is equal and unconditional, then our compassion will be immeasurable and impartial. When we accomplish this, we will pervade all directions with awareness imbued with *equanimity*.

In the Western Pure Land of Amitabha Buddha, there are uncountable bodhisattvas, beings who are dedicated to helping all others end suffering. Widely known in this world and often depicted standing to Amitabha's left is Avalokitesvara, or Guanyin Bodhisattva. Avalokitesvara is often translated as "Great Compassion Bodhisattva" or "She who hears the cries of the world."

A very long time ago, Avalokitesvara vowed that if she ever became disheartened in saving sentient beings, may her body shatter into a thousand pieces. Once, after liberating countless beings from the hell realms by teaching them the Dharma, she looked back down into the hell realms. To her horror, she saw that the hell realms were quickly filling up again!

In a fleeting moment of despair, she felt profound grief. And in that moment, in accordance with her vow, her body shattered into a thousand pieces. She beseeched the Buddhas to help and many did. Like a fall of snowflakes they came. One of those Buddhas was Amitabha. He and the other Buddhas helped to re-form her body into one that had a thousand arms and hands, with an eye of wisdom in each hand. In this way, she could better help all sentient beings.

Whether you view this as a true account or a legend, there is a very important lesson here that can help us in our practice of compassion. When we first develop the bodhi mind—the mind set on helping all beings attain enlightenment, ourselves included—we will experience times when we are disheartened. At this point, we have two choices: go forward or give up. To go forward, we need to reestablish our confidence. We may do this under the guidance of a good teacher, through the support of a good spiritual friend, or through other means. If we do not go forward, we will fall back into ignorance and delusion.

It will help us at these difficult times to remember that we do not grow spiritually in good times, when everything is going our way. We grow spiritually and progress on the path of awakening in times of adversity. Just as steel is tempered by fire, our resolve is strengthened by hardship.

Avalokitesvara was shattered in a fleeting moment of despair. But through the strength of her aspiration to help all beings, she touched the hearts of those who had gone before her on the path. Due to her great vow and profound sincerity, she had created the causes for many Buddhas to help her when she was momentarily overwhelmed by the enormity of her chosen task. We too will encounter obstacles. When we do, our aspiration to help all beings will enable us to receive the help we need to move back onto the path.

Due to the depth of her vow to help, Avalokitesvara regarded all beings with equanimity. In the above story, in addition to the hell realms, she also went to the ghost, animal, human, demi-god, and heavenly realms teaching all those who had the affinity to learn from her. Each being was equally important, and so she taught each one as best she could. She did not discriminate and was not judgmental. She tirelessly and vigilantly listened for cries for help and found the beings who were suffering. She then taught them so they were able to advance on the path to awakening.

With similar equanimity, we too will view everything equally and in a balanced way. Often when we try to help others, we act impulsively and erratically, not wisely. We rush in to help one day and then feel like giving up the next. Without a pure, calm mind, we can lose our balance and fall from great enthusiasm to mind-numbing discouragement. Only when our minds are calm will we know how to truly benefit others.

The Buddha told an account of how a father saved his children from a burning house. Some children were playing inside a very large, old house. They were so engrossed in their play that they did not realize the house was on fire. Their father called out frantically for them to leave the house, but unable to hear him, they continued playing. Luckily, he had the presence of mind to call out to the children that there were newly-arrived carts outside the house, something the children had been looking forward to. On hearing that the carts had arrived, they rushed out of the house to see them and, in so doing, were saved from the fire.

On a very basic level, this account shows how by using our calm, clear mind, we can more effectively determine the best way to help others. By running into the house, the father would have perished in the fire with his children. By remaining calm, he acted from his innate wisdom and saved them.

In our practice of compassion and equanimity, we also need patience. Patience is one of the virtues that bodhisattvas practice to perfection. Avalokitesvara needed great patience to teach all the beings and then even greater patience to continue helping them after that moment of despair. The father needed patience to hold himself back from a foolish act. Thinking calmly, he found a way to save his children. We too need patience to be compassionate and to regard all with equality.

We need patience to help us get through emotional and physical obstacles when we try to help others. There will always be obstacles. Just because we are trying to help does not guarantee that all obstacles will fall away and everything will be resolved to our satisfaction. Remember, we cannot overcome the karma of others and the ensuing retributions. Without patience, we will be mired in the quagmire of our own disappointment.

Also, without patience, we will give up when criticized and obstructed by those who do not understand what we are trying to do. Just as we sincerely believe that we have wisely found the way to help, others will likewise be certain that they, too, have the right solution. If we are prepared for this and do not allow it to disturb our serenity, we will not be shaken from our pure, calm mind.

As we encounter criticism and obstacles that seem overwhelming, we will need patience. Everything changes—good and bad, pleasant and unpleasant. Remember that just as good times do not last forever, bad times will also change and improve. Although our current conditions may seem overwhelmingly distressing, even these difficulties will some day end. If we can manage to hold on to this thought, we will find the patience within us to persevere, to hold on until our unfavorable conditions begin to ease.

This turnaround will take place more quickly if we can manage to let go of thoughts of our own discomfort and disappointment. Think, instead, of how to end the distress of others. The sooner their distress ends, the sooner ours will end, for the pain of others is our pain as well. We are all one, all interconnected with one another.

Do not get sidetracked by thinking that the concerns of another are trivial, for to that person those concerns are all consuming and very important. How we feel about the validity of their concerns is unimportant. We should put personal judgments aside and instead focus on trying to alleviate their distress and unhappiness, which to them is very real.

How can others be happy? In the same way that we become happy: by leaving negative emotions behind. If we can show others how to be less engrossed in their emotional reactions, we will help them begin to react more from reasoning. If we can help them see that the underlying causes of unhappiness are attachment and aversion, we will have helped end someone's pain. By letting go of craving and aversion, one will realize that the cause of happiness is goodwill, compassion, and equanimity.

There are some things in life that we can change. It is our responsibility to try to alter them for the better. But sometimes, we will not be able to effect any change. If we can move from our personal sense of sorrow or regret over not being able to help directly, the gentle happiness that arises from our wish to help will still bring relief to others.

Be happy helping. And be content knowing that sometimes all we can do is to wish for others to be happy as well.

APPRECIATION

In the sutras, we often hear of gratitude. The prac-tice of gratitude is very important in Buddhism. But so often, we forget about feeling grateful. When things go our way and we receive what we desire, we congratulate ourselves and all too easily slip into arrogance. We forget about all those who have helped us get to where we are, allowing us to enjoy what we have. When we do not receive what we desire, we blame others! We forget that what we receive in life is due to our own causes and condi-tions, our own merits or lack of merits. But arrogance and blaming others are both afflictions and, thus, are obstacles to our progress on the path to awakening.

If instead, we are grateful for all the help we have received from others, in our happiness, we will in turn want to share what we have with others. When Buddhists share, they dedicate their merits—the goodness they create every day—to four benefactors. These four are the Three Jewels, our parents, our teachers, and all beings. We mention these four in our Dedication of Merit, which begins "May the merits and virtues accrued from this work adorn the Buddha's Pure Land, [and] repay the Four Kindnesses above."

The Three Jewels are the Buddha, the Dharma, and the Sangha. They are called jewels because they are of immeasurable value. All Buddhas strive to teach us universal truths that will enable us to awaken—to uncover the true nature within each of us and escape suffering and attain happiness. Their determination to help us as well as their patience in teaching us is infinite. While our love for others is transitory, the Buddhas' love for all beings is endless. Our love is conditional and discriminatory, but the Buddhas' love is unconditional and held equally for all beings.

Buddhas help us by teaching us the principles of reality, principles such as causality; the impermanence of all conditioned phenomena; the non-existence of a permanent, independent self; and the interconnectedness of everything that exists. In other words, they teach us the universal, eternal laws of the cosmos—the Dharma. When we truly comprehend these teachings, we will then be able to eliminate our mistaken views and, instead, have right views and correct understanding. When we do not have such understanding, we will continue to wander aimlessly throughout countless lifetimes, immersed in our ignorance and delusion.

We improve our understanding and practice the teachings with the support of the Sangha, the community of those who practice the teachings. With the help of good friends on the path, we strive to attain purity of mind and to live lives of harmony. The pure mind is the mind that has no wandering thoughts and discriminations. It has no worries, no attachments, no thoughts of like or dislike. To live lives of harmony is to be gentle and caring in our thoughts and behavior.

We express our gratitude to the Three Jewels by endeavoring to practice as the Buddhas have taught us. How? By being content with the circumstances we find ourselves in. By listening to what the other person is saying, instead of being pre-occupied with our own self-interest. By empathizing with the pain and disappointment in the lives of those we encounter. Ultimately, we express our gratitude by awakening to correct views and understanding, attaining purity of mind, and living in harmony with all beings. In this way, we will begin to repay our immense debt to the Three Jewels for all their patience and help.

Second, we should be grateful to our parents. Many of us are or have been fortunate enough to have loving parents who tried their very best for us. Others, unfortunately, have or had parents who were less than ideal or even abusive. As Buddhists, we believe that we are drawn to our parents because of karmic connections. After death and before our next birth, we are plunged into darkness and raw emotions. In that overwhelming confusion, we are pulled to our parents as if they were a tiny beacon of light piercing that darkness.

There are four reasons that we are drawn to and born to our parents: to repay a kindness, to have kindness repaid to us, to repay a debt, or to exact repayment of a debt.

The child who is well behaved when young and loving when grown, and who affectionately tends to

the parents' needs and wishes is repaying past kindness. The parent who tenderly cares for the infant
and who does everything he or she can to provide for
the growing child's physical and emotional needs is
repaying kindness to the child. The unselfish care of
both the attentive child and the caring parents in
these two examples is natural and freely given. The
attention and nurturing continue as long as the kindness from an earlier lifetime is yet to be repaid and
the thoughtfulness yet to be returned.

On the other hand, the child who owes a debt to
the parent may well spend a lifetime trying to please
or provide for the parent. Although the parent may
not acknowledge and may even put down the child's
efforts, the child will continue to repay the debt that
he or she owes from an earlier lifetime. Whatever the
debt may be, the repayment could be financial or
entail physical effort, or it could take other forms.

The child who comes to exact repayment of a debt
may cause the parent endless worry and pain by
being disobedient or demanding. They may fall ill
frequently or have an ongoing medical condition and
need much attention and care from the parent.

Regardless of the reason we are born to our parents and regardless of their treatment of us, we still owe our parents an immense debt of gratitude. Even if our parents did nothing else for us, and most parents do not fall into this category, at the very least they provided us with the physical opportunity to be born. For nine months, our mothers carried and nurtured us until we reached the time of birth. They then underwent many hours of pain to bring us safely into this world. For many of us, our parents looked after us for years, sacrificing their personal comfort so we might have better lives than theirs.

But if our parents did not care for and nurture us, and if all they did was to give us our body and thus our life, we still cannot repay our debt of gratitude to them. Without them, we would not be here today striving to learn how to be more compassionate, altruistic beings.

So whatever the reasons we were born to our parents, whatever the circumstances we grew up in, however we feel about our parents, our debt to them is immeasurable.

Once we feel appreciation for our current parents, we next need to broaden our minds and hearts. In the *Brahma Net Sutra*, the Buddha said we should always bear in mind that "all male beings have been my father, all female beings have been my mother." Gradually, our appreciation should be felt for all beings throughout all time and space.

If our parents of this lifetime are no longer alive, we can still try to repay our debt to them by caring for all others as our parents by wanting them to be happy and loving them as if they were our own parents. Appreciate all others for the opportunities they provide for you to grow. Help all beings to feel cherished and safe in your presence. Say thank you at every opportunity.

If we are deeply appreciative of our present parents for this opportunity to learn and grow, and deeply appreciative of every one of our past parents, we will be able to feel gratitude towards all beings.

Third, we should be grateful to our teachers, those who have gone before us on the path to awakening. Until we reach a higher level of awakening, we will continue to act out of ignorance and delusion, mistaking right for wrong and wrong for right. If we are fortunate enough to have a good teacher, he or she will be able to guide us along the path. A good teacher will understand who we are and what we are capable of. This will enable our teachers to guide us wisely. Like the Buddhas, they will not give up on us when we fail to do all that we should.

But to find our good teacher, we need the right conditions. If the conditions have not yet matured, we could drive past the street every day where the teacher was and not know he or she was there. On the other hand, when the conditions are right, we will naturally meet our teacher. It is said, "When the student is ready, the teacher will appear." In other words, when conditions are right, it will happen.

One day when I was to give a lecture at a library in Lawrence, Kansas, a man who was returning some books saw the poster for my talk. Amazed, he went up to one of the organizers and said that he had wanted to take the three refuges but did not know any monastics. After the talk, at his request, I served as the witness in his ceremony of taking the refuges. He was very moved and deeply grateful. His conditions to formally follow the Buddhist path had matured. He had never expected to walk into that library and find a Buddhist nun! In the same manner, when our conditions are right, we will meet our teacher.

If we have not yet found our teacher, we need to plant the causes to do so. Helping and caring for others, studying and practicing our chosen Buddhist method, and having the wish to benefit all beings will all help to plant good seeds, which will mature into good conditions.

   We will instinctively know when we have found our teacher. This realization will occur in our prajna wisdom, our intuitive wisdom that is already deep within us. If we are fortunate enough to find our teacher, we will be able to learn quickly from him or her. We will have confidence in and happily follow what he or she teaches.

   If we are not yet fortunate enough to have found our teacher, we can use the sutras—the teachings of the Buddhas—as our teacher. We respectfully call Sakyamuni Buddha our "original teacher." "Original" means that within our current age, Sakyamuni Buddha is our historical Buddha. He is by no means the first and only Buddha, as there have been infinite Buddhas before him and there will be infinite Buddhas in the future. The teachings in the sutras flowed from the true nature of Shakyamuni Buddha. This true nature is the same true nature of all

Buddhas, of all beings. Such teachings are timeless.

By practicing what we have been taught, we show gratitude to our teachers. What do we practice? We need to let go of greed and craving: we only need enough money to be safe and healthy, and to meet our responsibilities. Let go of anger and frustration: we do not have to react out of our negative habits by shouting at our children or the person who is not doing what we wish. Let go of ignorance and delusion: remember that the person next to you wants only what you want—to be happy and free of worry.

Fourth, we should have appreciation for and be grateful to all beings. Everyone and everything is interconnected. Nothing exists on its own. When we were young, our family supported us and our friends looked after us. As we grew up, we went to schools built by the communities we lived in. Then as now, our country protected us through the armed forces and emergency services personnel. Living in a country with the freedom to choose our faith tradition— our standard for ethical living—we are able to not just merely survive but to grow spiritually and emotionally.

This book that you are reading or the recording

that you are listening to came about through the hard work of many people. Many of these people were in turn supported by other people, perhaps financially, perhaps emotionally, who were in turn supported by the efforts of countless others. This interconnectivity goes on and on. Understanding that we do not live solely on our own, that no man is an island, we will begin to develop a sense of gratitude to all the infinite beings who help us to live better, more meaningful lives.

But what of those who have harmed us? Do we need to be grateful to them too?

Ideally, we should also be grateful to those who have harmed us, not just those we like and who care for us. Remember, we reap what we sow. Our lives today are the results of our past karmas of thoughts, words, and actions. There is no one else to blame when we experience unpleasant circumstances. Those who have harmed us are simply bringing us the consequences of our past karmas. We can do as we have always done: complain and become angry. Or we can choose to understand what is happening and accept that we have a karmic debt to repay. Gradually, we will even be able to feel grateful to those who harm us. Those who harm us provide us with an opportunity to repay a debt that we had incurred.

FOUR ASSURANCES

One time, when the Buddha was in Kalama, he spoke to the people there about the poisons of greed, anger, and ignorance. He explained that one who is a student of the Buddhas, and who is free of the three poisons and who pervades everything and every being throughout the cosmos with boundless loving-kindness, compassion, appreciation, and equanimity will be free from greed and hostility, and will thus be pure. This student will gain four assurances in this lifetime.

To appreciate fully what the Buddha told the people of Kalama, we need to know the requirements for a person to receive the four assurances. The Buddha said the first requirement was to eliminate greed, anger, and ignorance. Eliminating these three poisons was discussed in the third talk in this series.

The second requirement was to learn how to live

as the Buddha had taught. His students should live lives of goodwill and show loving-kindness to all beings. They should regard all beings and conditions with equanimity, and neither feel pulled by what they want nor be averse to what they dislike. In this way, their thoughts toward others would be imbued with loving-kindness, compassion, appreciation, and equanimity.

Such people feel deep concern and sympathy for all beings because they realize that all beings wish to be free of fear and suffering. Most people do not know how to eliminate fear and suffering because they do not know what causes them. The cause of both their fear and suffering is craving. Therefore, to eliminate fear and suffering we need to eliminate craving. When craving is eliminated, true happiness will arise.

True happiness is not happiness as we usually think of it. All beings wish for true happiness, but few know what it is, let alone how to achieve it. Ordinary happiness is that which is caused by craving, just as fear and suffering are caused by craving. True happiness arises when craving no longer exists. It is timeless and arises spontaneously from our true nature. It is the happiness of awakened beings.

Cause and effect permeate our lives. There is no escaping this universal law. When a person has done something wrong, there will be retribution now or later. No one can elude this retribution even though they may seem to be doing so now.

Understanding this, we should not be concerned about the behavior of others because we have no way of controlling others. We just need to focus on our own behavior. We can only hope to control ourselves. And in so doing, by following the teachings, we will eliminate the poisons of greed, anger, and ignorance.

Those who eliminate the three poisons and who follow the teachings have great compassion for those who are still suffering. Empathizing with the distress and unhappiness of others, they view all beings with limitless and impartial loving-kindness. They wish to help all beings, not just those they like or approve of, find lasting happiness and liberation. And with this wish to help all beings, they will come to understand that to successfully aid others they need to use skillful means because everyone has different abilities and conditions. Some people may wish to hear the teachings. Some will best be helped by being shown good examples, while others just need understanding and a kind word.

Awakened beings will view all beings nonjudgmentally and will interact with them unconditionally. We, on the other hand, continually judge others and usually find them lacking. We foolishly have expectations of others and thus set ourselves up for disappointment. We would be much happier without any expectations.

Most of us are not unconditional in what we do; we set conditions or have expectations. Most of the time, we are not even aware that we are doing this. For example, perhaps we will help others as long as they conform to our wishes. But if they fail to perform as we expect them to, we may feel disappointed. Or perhaps we will help someone as long as we find it convenient to do so. But when helping requires us to really go out of our way, we lose interest.

Fortunately, "those who practice the teachings" do not judge others. They have no hidden agendas laden with conditions. Thoughts of self-interest do not arise. They have let go of attachments as well as aversions. Thoughts of like and dislike will not arise. Thoughts that they are being inconvenienced or taken advantage of do not arise. And even when it requires more time and effort than they had planned on, they are able to remain enthusiastic about helping others.

The Buddha said a "noble disciple" who is free of the three poisons and who keeps pervading everything and every being in the cosmos with boundless loving-kindness, compassion, appreciation, and equanimity will receive four assurances.

The first assurance is if there is rebirth and retributions from good or ill karmas, then through his good karmas, he will have a good rebirth. The second assurance is if rebirth does not exist, he will be happy in this lifetime, as he will feel neither greed or anger nor their attendant suffering.

The third assurance is if a person who commits bad karmas suffers the related retributions, the noble disciple will not suffer because he will never give rise to bad thoughts, utter bad words, or commit any bad actions. The fourth assurance is if a person who commits bad karmas does not suffer the related retributions, then the noble disciple is purified anyway.

The first assurance is based on the existence of rebirth and causality. If one commits wrongdoing, then one will have a bad rebirth. If one does good deeds, one will have a good rebirth. It is because of this premise that many people strive to live a moral, selfless, and caring life. We all wish to end our suffering and to find happiness. But an awakened being, who has eliminated the three poisons and who is thoughtful and caring, goes one step further—he wishes to help others eliminate suffering and attain happiness as well.

It is difficult to be a truly compassionate person. It takes many, many lifetimes to become such a person. Believing in the reality of karma and rebirth, we understand that immorality and selfishness will lead us to miserable rebirths, rendering us unable to help ourselves or others. We have already wasted more lifetimes than we can count. Failing to practice the Buddha's teachings, we will waste many more. The only way to truly help people is to create and accumulate good fortune. Good fortune includes a safe place to live, enough material resources, skills, wisdom, time, and good health. These are the conditions found in a good rebirth. But only by using our good conditions to benefit others can we continue to generate more good conditions for future use. If we selfishly use the goodness we have created to make our own lives more pleasurable and neglect the needs of others, we will exhaust that goodness and subject ourselves to negative situations and suffering.

In the second assurance, the Buddha postulated a scenario contrary to his experience—one where there is no rebirth and no karmic retribution. He did this so that those who were doubtful could still benefit from his teachings.

He showed that even within such a scenario, one who remains free of greed, anger, and their resultant suffering will be truly happy!

Today, this assurance is especially helpful as people ask if they have to accept the existence of rebirth before they can benefit from the practice. As the Buddha showed, they do not have to accept rebirth in order to reap the benefits. Those who are free of greed, anger, and their ensuing suffering have a mind of loving-kindness, compassion, appreciation, and equanimity in this lifetime. They no longer experience greed, no longer crave the emotional high from acquiring that which is new—they simply appreciate what they already have. Craving and its shadow, disappointment, are eliminated as people become contented with their situation. This is true happiness.

We can only imagine how wonderful it would be to never again crave sensations and experiences—to appreciate what we already have.

And imagine never again feeling angry or unsettled but always feeling calm and peaceful instead. Such a person would surely always be happy and be at ease, and thus always be welcomed wherever he or she goes. Without craving and without anger there will be no suffering—just happiness, a lifetime of happiness. And all this can happen here and now, because even if one does not believe in rebirth, one will still benefit if one lives a life free of craving, animosity, and unhappiness.

The third assurance is if a person who commits bad karmas suffers the related retributions, the noble disciple will not suffer because he has no bad thoughts, speech, or actions. While those who commit wrongdoings will suffer the related effects, one who lives morally will not suffer because this person prevents bad thoughts, speech, and actions from occurring. In such a life, there will be no resultant suffering from having hurt another with harmful speech or actions. Such a person will have no reason to feel remorse. He will be free from worrying about how to undo what had been said or done out of carelessness and ignorance.

What are bad thoughts, speech, and actions? Bad thoughts arise from greed, anger, ignorance, arrogance, doubt, and wrong views. They harm others and us. When we fail to get what we want, we become angry. Craving and anger arise from our ignorance and from our lack of understanding. Arrogance and doubt also stem from ignorance. Wrong views compound our ignorance: not only do we not understand, we also hold mistaken ideas as correct!

Bad speech, that which is not correct, honest, and beneficial, harms others and us in several ways. False speech, by containing misinformation, is deceptive and leads people astray. Harsh speech destroys our peace of mind and that of everyone around us. Divisive speech separates people and fosters the seeds of conflict. Enticing speech cajoles people to do what they otherwise might not do.

What are bad actions? The Buddha gave us three precepts of no killing, no stealing, and no sexual misconduct. Killing is destroying another being's life, be it human or animal. Stealing is taking that which is not freely given to us. Sexual, or sensual, indulgence is the temporary seeking of pleasant sensations at the cost of our pure, calm mind.

One who lives life as taught by the Buddha does not have bad thoughts, use bad speech, or commit bad actions. Thus, this person's life is free of suffering. Such a person will know only contentment and peace of mind as his or her mind remains in a clear, tranquil state, free of agitation and fear.

The Buddha's fourth assurance is if a person who commits bad karmas does not suffer the related retributions, then the noble disciple is purified anyway because he no longer has any bad thoughts, speech, or actions.

Peace of mind comes to the person who lives morally. Having a pure mind, this person does not

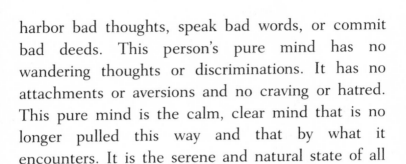

harbor bad thoughts, speak bad words, or commit bad deeds. This person's pure mind has no wandering thoughts or discriminations. It has no attachments or aversions and no craving or hatred. This pure mind is the calm, clear mind that is no longer pulled this way and that by what it encounters. It is the serene and natural state of all beings.

The Buddha provided four scenarios to help individuals learn how to eliminate that which is negative and harmful and to embrace that which is positive and valuable. Leading one's life in accordance with the Buddha's teachings, one will have a tranquil and stable mind. Pure in mind, one will also be pure in body as well, for the mind is the forerunner of one's actions. One who thus achieves a pure mind and body will enjoy the four kinds of assurances.

TRANSFORMING GREED AND ANGER

The Destructive Emotions of Greed and Anger

As human beings, we are subject to many negative habits, the most serious and detrimental of which are greed and anger. These stem from our emotional attachments to the concept of having an individual and permanent self, and to our lack of understanding about our true place in the universe and our relationships with all those who inhabit the universe with us.

Greed, or craving, arises from the mistaken idea that we can obtain and hold on to possessions, to ideas, and even to other people. Craving arises from selfishness, from the misconception that our bodies are who we are. But if we try to pinpoint where "I" actually exists in our bodies, we cannot do so. "I" cannot be found in the heart, in the head, or anywhere else in the body.

Every body is simply a combination of different

parts: two arms, two legs, many different organs including the brain and the heart—but none of them is "I." Not yet understanding this, we not only do everything we can to protect this body, but we also go to lengths to protect our possessions as well. We even believe in the need to defend our ideas, feeling threatened whenever someone disagrees with us.

The reality is that this body will only exist for a short time and that our possessions will be ours for an even briefer time, for we will take nothing with us at the end of this life. We know this reality all too well, but we still try to hold on dearly to whatever we have.

If you feel that this does not apply to you, please think of one of your most treasured possessions. Now, imagine giving away that treasured possession. How would you feel? If you are like most people, you will find it is very discomforting to think of no longer having such a valued possession.

This is a form of craving, as we desire to keep the things that we have and also acquire additional or new possessions. We convince ourselves that such possessions, even in the form of people and ideas, can make us happy.

But after we have acquired something new or obtained more of something we already have, we so often find ourselves wishing for another new object or perhaps for much more of what we just obtained. This is, unfortunately, human nature. Even young children demonstrate this as they do whatever is necessary, for example, to convince the adult with them to buy a new toy. Later, often in a matter of hours, the child loses interest and wants another new plaything.

We do the same thing; our toys are just larger and more expensive. But the principle is the same: Old or young, we are rarely satisfied and are, instead, often disappointed and, thus, often unhappy.

We will never find lasting and genuine happiness through possessions but will, instead, remain forever discontented. Not yet realizing this, we still feel that it is perfectly natural to want more and to accumulate more. We are even envious of others and maybe secretly hope to impress others with what we have.

This fault-ridden idea of "more is good" is buoyed up by an advertising industry constantly telling us that by purchasing what they are selling, we will find the answer to our prayers: happiness, love, youth, security—the list is endless. Feeling that we do not have enough happiness, love, youth, and security, we buy into their enticing pitches in the belief that their product or service will alleviate our nagging sense of discontent.

Clinging to the idea that the source of happiness lies outside ourselves, we become attached to things, places, and even ideas. We ignore the reality that nothing remains with us forever: possessions are lost or become unimportant, people leave us or we leave them, places are left behind, ideas change. Such attachments are why we are still living lives of unhappiness: because we cling to things, to ideas, to life. We desire—we want—all of these.

In our desire to possess, we even wish to possess other people. We want others to respect us and to love us. We want others to only think of us, to always come back to us, to forever be with us. This is a form of craving and a major attachment, which is due largely to not yet realizing that we are all impermanent: We all change from second to second. None of us remains the same. No one can forever hold on to what we now have.

Our lives are brief. Time seems to tick by so slowly when we are miserable. But when we are happy, that moment in our lives feels very short. Albert Einstein, while trying to explain the theory of relativity, put it into simple words that most of us can understand: If we put our hand on a hot stove for a few seconds, it will feel like eternity. But if you are a man sitting next to an attractive woman, ten minutes can feel like seconds. Everything is relative.

But even as brief as our lives are, nothing will remain with us forever. The person with us now will not always be with us. This is so painful for us because we become attached, in this case, to people whom we do not want to lose. When they are gone, we will miss them as we continue to think of them and the pleasant times we had together. But, for good or for bad, we cannot keep any person with us.

As Buddhists, we believe that we have been reborn innumerable times. In many of those lifetimes, we have cared deeply for others. In future lifetimes, this will happen again as our attachments pull us back into those relationships lifetime after lifetime. These attachments may be for places, for things, for ideas or people, and this time around they may spread over an entire lifetime, perhaps our current one. Or they may come rushing together in our final moments, overwhelming us.

When we are dying, we can be lead into many directions by our thoughts. These final thoughts are so crucial because they lead us to our next lifetime. I have, on different occasions, spoken with nurses, family members, and friends who were with people who were dying. One such person told me of what had happened to a friend of hers.

A few years ago, another nun and I were speaking weekly to a small group of friends. The first time we met with them, we learned of a friend of theirs who was very ill. Her time was spent between hospital and home. When she was in the hospital, the friends would talk to her about practicing Buddhism and trying to be a better person, but she would explain that she did not have the energy right then and would practice when she returned home. When they visited her at home after she left the hospital and again discussed Buddhism and urged her to be a kinder, more forgiving and honest person, she would say that she was healthier now and would get around to such things later.

As we continued to meet with the group, we learned that in the past when the friends would go out shopping, the one who was now sick would invariably say that she had forgotten her money and would then ask to borrow some from the others. It was also a habit of hers to forget to repay what she had borrowed. The friends were understandably upset about this but they also knew that their friend still needed support and encouragement to accept and benefit from Buddha's teachings.

One day, when the woman was in the hospital again, one of the friends visited her. As she was lying there, she began to tell her visitor about a time when she had loaned another person some money and jewelry. As she was bitterly and angrily complaining that this person had failed to return the jewelry, the woman suddenly died. The friend who had been with her told us that the woman's face was contorted with anger when she died. And within thirty minutes, her face turned a very dark gray.

What we are feeling in our final moments will lead us to our next lifetime. If we are calm as we are dying, that calmness will lead us to our next lifetime. If we are very angry, then anger will lead us into the next lifetime. We may not be able to prove where this woman was reborn, but her appearance right after she died was dire indeed. She died this way because of anger and craving.

She was not thinking of the kindness of the friend who had come to visit her, or of the thoughtfulness of all the other friends who regularly visited her every time she entered the hospital—all those who wanted to help her become a better person. She was not thinking of any of that. Nor was she thinking of the nurses and doctors who were trying to help her and to ease her pain. She was thinking of her missing jewelry and she was indulging in her anger. As Buddhists, we are taught that anger will lead one to be reborn in the hell realms and that greed will lead one to be reborn in the hungry ghost realm.

The hungry ghost realm is a realm where beings have insatiable desires. They are constantly hungry and thirsty. Their stomachs are immense, but their throats are tiny and, so, they are unable to satisfy their hunger and thirst, unable to quench their desires. Notwithstanding whether one believes that the hell and hungry ghost realms are in other dimensions or whether they exist now in this world, we are led to them because of our anger and craving.

Our greed and craving tie us to unhappiness and lead us to so much harmful behavior. Because of craving, we become angry as others take or have something we want. Greed can also be there in the act of giving should we continue to think about the object we have given away, because our mind still clings to it.

Greed is one of our most severe problems, but there is a way to counteract our greed. It is the first of the six perfections that Bodhisattvas, who are awakened beings, practice.

The Giving of One's Self and Possessions

To counteract our craving, we can practice generosity. Think again of giving away that treasured possession. Do you think that you might miss it and wish that you had not given it away? Ideally, when we give something to others, we want to do so without a lengthy analysis, including such thoughts as to whether or not we like the receivers of the gift or whether they may or may not deserve getting it. Upon seeing somebody needing an object that we have, we can simply offer the object to the person.

Genuine generosity is to spontaneously and unconditionally offer what we have when we believe that it will make the recipient happy. We do so without having second or remorseful thoughts. After such giving, we strive to let go of the thought that we had given and that of the object given.

When we practice generosity, we can start out with something that is not a favorite item, and from that we continue giving. We live in an affluent world and many of us have more than we need. We only need a modest amount of clothes to keep us comfortable and to protect us from inclement weather. We only need a reasonable size home. We can live very healthily on simple, wholesome foods. We really do not need a lot. Instead of clinging to every item that we have, we can practice generosity.

Initially, if you find generosity difficult, start by giving something that you have not used for a while, say a year or two. Doing so, most people will realize they do not have any regrets or feel a sense of loss. On the contrary, most of us will instead feel good because we have helped another person. We have given away an article of not much use to us and, in doing so, helped someone else.

Eventually, we will unconditionally and spontaneously offer the things that we do use and treasure when we feel the other person needs it more than we do. Afterwards, if we happen to think about the object, we will still feel happy and glad that we had given it to another.

Even if the recipients use the item for only a short time, we will gradually accept that we have practiced genuine generosity and had made an offering of happiness. From this giving we can be contented. And even if they never use it again or pass it to another, we can remain happy knowing that we have begun to reduce our clinging, that we are one tiny step closer to severing all of our attachments, one tiny step closer to awakening to the innate goodness within each of us.

What about those who are unable to give possessions because they have very little? For those who may just have enough to provide food, shelter, and the basic necessities for their families, what can they do if there is nothing extra to give to others? Not having excess material resources does not preclude us from giving, for we can also give of our abilities and time. All forms of giving allow us to counteract our craving—this is just another way to do so. How many times has somebody asked us for help to do something? And how many times have we excused ourselves by saying that we were very tired but, in reality, we just wanted to stay home and relax, or maybe watch television?

And what if we had helped? How many of us had thought, "I wonder how soon I can leave. This work is very difficult and when I am finally finished, I'm going to be exhausted and won't have time for myself. I wish I had stayed home."

This is a form of greed. This is thinking that this body—our body—is important, that keeping our body comfortable is important, perhaps more important than helping someone else.

To counteract this kind of greed, we can practice generosity. We all probably know excellent examples of people who do this, people whom we admire and whom we wish we were like. Upon seeing that somebody needs assistance, these people automatically help the other person. It just seems so natural for them to do so—an effortless act.

When we spend some time to think about it, we will realize this kind person was probably even more tired than we were, but was able to do so much more than we did, or wanted to, and seemingly without getting tired or disgruntled. They looked happy doing exactly what they were doing, which was helping someone else. This is genuine generosity.

We, too, will be overcoming our greed when we can help others spontaneously. If we persevere, the day will arrive when we will be able to help people without waiting to be asked, when we will just do so without any prompting. This practice takes time to develop, but gradually we will improve.

We can also practice giving when upon seeing somebody who is upset, we walk up and simply smile at them or say a few thoughtful words. Doing so, we instinctively provide them with what they need to feel better. And it might be at a moment when we ourselves, very honestly, might not have felt like smiling or being insightful, and perhaps even felt like we were the ones needing a smile or kind word. But frankly, helping others will be more beneficial than being helped—always.

When we are able to give in this way—when we learn to give as caring and generous people give—we will no longer feel tired. And even if we feel tired when we begin helping, after a while we will find that giving makes us feel more alert, happy, and energetic. We will no longer be worried by what had been troubling us before. By concentrating on helping others, we will no longer be upset by negative feelings that seem to be constantly bombarding us. This is the result of sincerely giving to others.

The Giving of Teaching

We can also give by teaching. We may not have many objects to give. But most people are good at doing things that others are not, or may know things that others do not know. We can impart to others whatever skills and knowledge we have. We do not need to have exceptional skills or special knowledge. We just teach others who wish to learn so that they too will acquire those skills or understanding.

When we see someone who is in need, perhaps, of food or other basic necessities, we can first give them what they need to meet their immediate needs, but then we can go a step further by finding ways to teach them what they need to know to become self-sufficient. This way, they can also care for those they love and are responsible for.

In our teaching, however, we should not withhold any information, but continue teaching all that we know, as long as the person wishes to learn. If, due to our selfishness, we decide to not teach the other person to the best of our ability by sharing all that we know, or perhaps due to self-interest, we decide that we have done enough and that the other person can figure out the rest himself, then we are not sincerely teaching. Sincerity is the key. We may not know a lot, but as long as we know something that others do not, then we should openly and honestly share our skills and knowledge with them.

Even if we do not have possessions or knowledge to give, we can still be kind. We can still be respectful to others. We can still be considerate of all beings around us. We can help others to feel safe around us.

The Giving of Fearlessness

Another way we can give is to relieve the worries and fears of others. A friend told me of an incident that had occurred in her home. A caring woman with an excellent sense of humor, she does draw the line at some things. Upon walking into her bathroom, she saw a large python on the floor. Having good reflexes, she drew the line and firmly closed the door. Knowing she was not at risk, her immediate thought was for her elderly cat that could no longer move quickly.

Jenny, who is Buddhist by practice, called to her husband, Rob, who is Buddhist at heart. Rob looked in the phone book and located a snake catcher. However, before the snake catcher was allowed to leave the premises with his catch, Rob thoughtfully queried the gentleman: Was the snake okay? How would it be released and where? Would it be safe or would it be subject to any risk? The snake catcher patiently explained that he would take it a considerable distance away before he would release it in a safer and more natural environment. My two caring friends watched while the snake catcher carefully checked the python, then assured them that it had not suffered any from its capture and that it would be fine in a safer habitat.

How many of us would have taken the time, made the effort, and gone to the expense that was involved in catching and saving the snake? This was a case of the giving of safety and of caring for the welfare of others, even when the "other" is a six-foot python. This is an ideal example of helping other beings feel safe around us because this offering of fearlessness and safety was not given to only one being—the cat—but also to all beings involved, including the snake.

Every thought we have is instantly felt by all others throughout the universe, for we are all one—we are all inter-related. We just do not yet realize this because we have not experienced this oneness. In the above example of the snake, the thought was to protect one life without harming the other. That thought, of compassion and loving-kindness, was felt by all beings whether they were in the house with the snake or on the other side of the universe.

Many people who find themselves in this situation probably would have thought, "To protect my cat, I will kill the snake." But Jenny and Rob's thoughts did not come from attachment to their cat or from the desire to protect what was theirs. Rather, their thoughts arose spontaneously from the reverence held equally for all forms of life and their wish to provide security and safety.

When we, too, begin to give with compassion and understanding, we will gradually feel a sense of contentment and happiness. In time, we will be able to look at a treasured possession without feeling attached to it and think, "I know who would really like this." And, in time, as our giving becomes more natural, we will find that, more and more, our spontaneous giving is accompanied by fewer thoughts of what we have just done.

Lives of Happiness and Freedom

Buddhist teachings can be subsumed into three phrases:

Avoid all that is bad,
Embrace all that is good,
Purify the mind.

To live lives of happiness and freedom, we need to "eradicate all that is bad." We need to curtail—and eventually eliminate—our craving, desires, and attachments because they lead the way to so many of our negative emotions and bad habits. We will experience lifetimes upon lifetimes of unhappiness if we allow them to make us cling to possessions, people, etc.

As we work to "embrace all that is good," a good place to start is the eradication of our greed through giving and generosity. We will feel the happiness from giving something to another. Gradually, we will find ourselves thinking less of the elation we feel after having done something for another. Eventually, we will just find ourselves offering spontaneously and no longer even thinking about what we have done. We will find, instead, that we naturally maintain a quiet and serene state of happiness.

As we let go of attachments, at some point we will no longer become upset but will remain calm and content when we encounter things not working out as we hope. This ideal response will happen infrequently at first, but gradually we will react this way more often. Conversely when things do go the way we want, we will again remain calm and content instead of proud or desirous in wanting the pleasantness to continue. The more we let go of selfishness and attachments, the more we will remain calm and content regardless of the circumstance. In this way, we will be learning how to "purify the mind."

Many of us will find that we can gradually manage not becoming upset at bad occurrences. But not wanting the good times to continue can be more difficult because it seems harmless. What is wrong with wanting tomorrow to be as good as today? While this thinking does not harm others, it can inadvertently harm us for we are attaching or clinging to good times. This is still a form of greed.

What we are aiming at is to remain calm and content—to be unattached—at all times. Yes, this is extremely difficult at first and may well seem impossible. But with enthusiasm and effort, very gradually, we will find that whether things do not go our way or on those unusual times when they do, we will remain calm and content either way.

So often it seems that other people want to do something differently from the way we want to do it. When others want to go one way and we want to go another, this is the very time that we need to be not attached to our way of doing things. If their preference is not morally wrong but just another way of doing something, try to go along with it. Becoming upset and making everyone uncomfortable will not help anyone. Try and remember two contrasting occasions, one that had you fuming and another in which you were extremely happy. Which feels better? Do not give in to the old negative habits: Find a more reasonable way of reacting.

A cost-free, painless, and instantaneous way of re-acting is to smile. Even if there is no one around, we can smile. Initially when we try to do this, we will feel somewhat embarrassed should somebody walk into the room and find us sitting there just smiling to ourselves. They may look somewhat concerned at first, but as we sit there, smiling, they will very quickly feel like smiling too. So smile and be happy; others will feel it.

Feeling the happiness of others is far superior to picking up on other people's greed and selfishness. We do not feel comfortable with people who seem to radiate such negative feelings. Alternatively, when we are with others who are generous and always thinking of others, we feel happy just being near them.

As we practice generosity and start to eradicate our greed, others will notice. They may not say anything, but they will notice. And they will see that in sincere giving, both the one who gives and the one who receives benefit. This is how we can teach others without saying a word but by setting examples.

If someone tells us to give but they themselves do not give, we will not value what they say. On the other hand, if we see somebody who seems to not have much, but constantly gives things away—for example, somebody who only has a little bit of food, but who says, "Here, have this"—this is the person to learn from.

Greed is very ugly. It leads to many negative emotions. It leads us to endless lives of unhappiness because we try to selfishly protect ourselves, our possessions, our ideas, and our knowledge; and because we think our possessions, ideas, and knowledge are real and will make us happy. But our ideas, possessions, craving, desires, and attachments will not bring happiness.

Generosity will bring happiness. More than likely, we are not yet able to practice the level of generosity that we wish. But we can still begin where we are: We can teach others. Surely, each of us can smile at somebody else. Many of us have things that we can give to others, skills that can be used to benefit others, or time that can be used to help others.

In doing so, we will feel happy and we will begin to feel free. We will even begin to feel lighter because our attachments will start to drop away from us. But if we do not eliminate or at least reduce our greed, craving, and attachments, we will fall prey to an emotion that most of us have come to dread—anger.

The Seeds of Anger

Anger arises when greed is unrestrained; when we do not get what we want, because others reject our ideas or obtain what we had wanted for ourselves; or when what we have is taken from us, or those we love are lost to us. The ways that craving, desire, and attachments can overwhelm us and, then, lead us to anger are endless. The pain generated, as a consequence, is infinite.

Anger is one of our greatest problems. It arises before we even realize what is happening. Somebody says something and, in a flash, we are angry. It is too late to try to control the anger: It has already ignited. When this happens we can try to think about why we have become angry, where this anger really came from.

It did not start with this incident, nor did it start yesterday, last week, or last year. As Buddhists, we believe that it started many, many lifetimes ago. In the past, one of us said something to the other. We did not mean to hurt the other one's feelings; we just did not pay attention to what we were about to say. So we spoke carelessly and did not realize that something in what we had said hurt the other person.

But deep within the one we had upset, the incident was registered in that part of all of us that courses through each lifetime. When we next met, maybe in our next lifetime or maybe after a hundred lifetimes, that other person unconsciously remembered the pain of what had happened. This time, he said something to us and this time there was just a hint of resentment. After that, the incident again withdrew into both of our subconsciousnesses.

We continue to pass the anger back and forth each time we encounter one another. Each time, our mutual anger becomes stronger. Each time, as we act on that anger, our feelings intensified. Eventually, verbally lashing out at the other will not be enough: One of us will strike the other. But still it does not end.

Meeting again, we will get into a fight. Meeting yet again, fighting will not be enough as our need to seek retaliation—to hurt the other—will have intensified into an intense fury. Our desire for revenge will lead us to an inevitability: One of us will kill the other. But even this is not the end, for personal anger and desire for retaliation is not confined to individuals. Individual anger leads to territorial, ethnic, and religious conflicts. Conflicts lead to war, war to annihilation.

All of this anger, pain, and suffering came about because of one unnoticed thought, one careless word. We did not mean to hurt the other person; we just were not paying attention to what we were saying—this is how anger and hatred begin.

So the next time anger is being passed back and forth, as we become more embroiled in it, remember that we are not innocent victims in the latest spate of rage. We both have participated in this exchange, one which has gone on for longer than we can imagine; the other person is not the only one at fault. With this realization comes the thought that we can either continue fueling the anger or one of us can choose to stop what is happening by consciously letting go of the anger.

When we become angry, nothing positive is accomplished, nothing is resolved, nothing at all. If we respond in anger, that anger will grow more tenacious, more frightening. But responding with logic while the other person is angry may not help to diffuse the anger either.

Logic is, very often, the last thing an angry person wishes to hear. We have been there ourselves. Just try and remember the last time you were angry. How would you have reacted if the other person told you to calm down? It is very rare that a person can say to us "Please, do not be angry" with any real effect, especially when we are practically fuming.

So where is this anger that is so difficult to restrain stemming from? The anger is coming from within us, not from the other person. We are making ourselves angry by allowing the other person to "push our buttons" and to infuriate us—we are doing it to ourselves.

Being cognizant of this, we can choose, instead, to let go of the anger. Maybe we can choose not to say anything else right away. Maybe we can count to ten or take deep breaths. Maybe, instead of replying angrily to them, we can simply say "Amituofo." Maybe we can say nothing, or if nothing else seems to work, we can quietly withdraw.

Usually, in this way, the other person's anger will die down more quickly because we are not responding to them. Later on, we can try talking to them. We could ask what we did to upset them and possibly apologize for having done so. Often, all the other person needs to hear is "I'm sorry"; this may be enough to control, reduce, or diffuse the anger on their part.

Anger makes us miserable, guilty, and upset, as we cannot sleep or concentrate. More than likely, the other person feels equally unhappy, upset, and unsettled. Out of compassion for the other person, we should do what we can to try and reduce this anger, to try to resolve what is going on between us. If we cannot do so, if we cannot find a way to eradicate—to stop—what is happening, we might try to avoid the person for a while or avoid the circumstance that seems to trigger the hostility.

Also, we can think about what happened in this instance—what we did that contributed to the other person as well as ourselves becoming angry—and, then, we can resolve how to act more judiciously in the future.

Affinities and Enmities

From all our past lifetimes, the people we encountered are more than we can count. Some of these relationships had been good ones, while others, unfortunately, had been bad ones. Sometimes, when we encounter people we had known before, we "recognize" them. Most of us have had the occasional experience whereupon meeting someone, we felt like we were meeting an old friend. In a sense, we were. We felt like we could have sat down and talked for hours, and maybe we did. Whenever we are with such an "old friend," we feel happy and relaxed. This is a good affinity, a natural, positive connection with another person.

Conversely, we all probably have also had the experience of meeting someone and instantly feeling an immediate dislike for that person. The individual did not say anything offensive, perhaps only said "Hello," but we still felt a strong dislike. Whenever we encounter our "old antagonist," we feel uncomfortable and tense. These are enmities, or negative affinities from our past.

When we encounter someone with whom we have a negative affinity, we can remind ourselves that, very possibly, we are irritating him just as he is irritating us. Why have we ended up in this situation? Karma. Karma is literally an "action." Our thoughts, speech, and physical behavior plant causes. Everything that happens in our lives today is almost entirely the result of the causes we planted in our past lifetimes. Very little of what is happening to us now is the result of what we did earlier in this current lifetime.

Since the causes were already created, there is nothing we can do to change them. We can, however, control the conditions that allow the causes to develop a result. For example, a seed is a cause that needs the right conditions to grow: good soil, adequate water, and plenty of sunshine. When these conditions are present, the seed can grow. But we can keep the seed from maturing by withholding the necessary conditions. Without soil, water, and sunlight, the seed cannot grow—the cause cannot mature—because the necessary conditions are absent. Therefore, if we cannot diffuse the anger by letting it go, we can try to control the conditions.

There is an account of a Buddhist who had attained a certain level of insight due to his years of cultivation. Having some ability to foresee what would happen in the future, he knew that in a certain city in China, an individual would kill him because he had killed that person in a previous lifetime. Knowing this, he also understood that although he had attained some achievement in his practice, he was not yet at the level where upon being killed he would not feel anger when this happened. Thus, he would not be able to control his emotions to avoid creating more negative karma.

However, by not going to that particular city, he could control the conditions. In this way, he was able to further continue his practice with sincerity and diligence. When he had reached the level where he would no longer give in to anger, he went to that particular city in China. He met the person and he was killed. But since he could control his emotions, he was able to stop the anger and hatred at that point.

He managed to practice to a point where he could control the conditions—a rare feat indeed. He did this not just for himself but for the other person as well, because he understood that if he gave rise to anger then he would, in turn, kill the other person in a future lifetime.

His actions required much more self-discipline than most of us possess. But we can still work at controlling conditions on a more modest level. If somebody constantly irritates us and all of our efforts to resolve the situation have failed, we can withdraw temporarily and go work on reducing our anger, with a goal of eliminating it. In this way, we can begin to control conditions.

Who Makes Us Angry?

We can also remind ourselves that other people do not make us angry—we ourselves do. When we encounter a difficult situation, we have a choice of how to react. We can carelessly fall into our usual habit of losing our temper, or we can react wisely. It is entirely up to us.

Why do we so easily become angry? We do so because we are attached to self-importance, our view of who we are, to the concept of "I." When our concept of "I" is threatened, "I" very often strikes out in anger.

A good example of this is the typical reaction to criticism. We have many faults, but we generally do not appreciate others pointing them out to us. Regardless, others very often criticize us, just as we are often critical of others. When somebody points out a fault, they, like us, usually do so clumsily, and consequently, our feelings are hurt. Few people are able to correct us or criticize us without us reacting negatively.

We respond defensively with resentment, guilt, embarrassment, or a score of other reactions. We may well know we have done something wrong, but we do not appreciate others pointing it out to us. We resent critiques because we feel that others are in no position to criticize us: Surely, they must have, sometime in the past, done what we just did and made the same mistake as us. Or we may find it difficult to apologize—no matter how guilty we feel—and so we react with anger or try to ignore the situation.

It is very difficult to accept others' criticism of us, and it is the rare person who would find it easy to say, "You are absolutely right. I apologize and will not do it again." Such humility coupled with strength of character is usually not readily found in most of us. More likely, we will act defensively or worse. We may, in turn, criticize the other person. So, let us think before we react.

There are two possibilities occurring whenever we receive criticism. The first possibility is, yes, we did or said something wrong. If we are unable to deal with this reality right away, perhaps we can retreat by ourselves or with a friend. Hopefully, on our own or with our friend's help, we can figure out how not to make the mistake again. Maybe we can try to be more aware of how others are reacting to us, or maybe we can try to think more before we speak or act. Whatever we decide to do, we must carry out with determination.

Instead of being angry or feeling guilty or becoming embarrassed, we can try to be grateful. After all, it is not they who had done something wrong—it was us—so becoming defensive and getting upset is rather futile. More importantly, we must realize that we have been provided an opportunity to improve and to be a better person in the future. For this we should be appreciative, not angry. This is the best response when we make a mistake and someone is helpful enough to bring it to our attention.

The second possibility is for someone to criticize us even if we have done nothing wrong. Being accused of doing something when we have not is even more likely to invoke anger. As quickly as possible, we need to get over our indignation. Whether the other person honestly thought we did something wrong, misunderstood what happened, or maybe exaggerated the circumstances is not the issue.

We can try to calmly clear things up, but whether or not we succeed, again, we have a choice as to how to respond. Knowing that anger resolves nothing, if we cannot help the other person to understand our position, we can at least try to let go of our anger. Aware of our mistake, we can try not to commit it in the future and let go of what has happened. We do not need to constantly go over the incident or feel sorry for ourselves that someone is giving us a difficult time. Simply forget about it—let it go.

If they criticize us and we did do what they said we did, they have pointed out one of our shortcomings, and we now know what we need to correct in the future. But if they have misjudged us and criticized us for something we have not done, then we must have done something in the past that brought this criticism about—perhaps we had unfairly criticized another, and our karma has caught up with us.

If we do not get upset, then we may be able to repay one karmic debt. If so, the person has just helped us and has, actually, done us a favor. If we can accept the situation and not get angry, become defensive or irritated, or feel anything negative, then this person has helped us to repay a karmic debt, of which we have an unimaginable amount. How can we become angry with someone who has helped us?

When a friend helps us, we appreciate their thoughtfulness: When does a reasonable person ever respond with anger? Never. Even if this friend was not doing something out of kindness, they are still helping us, still doing us a favor—something we can try to appreciate.

Yes, it is extremely difficult to view the situation this way, but gradually developing the ability to look at life's iniquities from this perspective will help us to become calmer and more contented. By criticizing us unfairly, those doing so have actually done us a kindness. If somebody has done something thoughtful for us, how can we become angry?

If, in the face of our trying to reason with our critics—and with a deep determination not to give in to anger—they continue to criticize us, there is no need to respond in kind or, even, in defense. If we respond by defending ourselves, we know what will happen. They say something, then we will say something. They will say, "Yes, you did." We will say, "No, I didn't." "Yes, you did." "No, I didn't." This goes on and on, with both of us becoming louder and angrier. Neither one of us is accomplishing anything, other than planting more seeds for criticism, unhappiness, and anger in the future. The other person may not realize what is going on, but we do because we have some understanding of karma and causality.

Everything arises from the mind. What we say and do now will determine what happens in our future. If we argue, we plant the seeds for acrimony in our future. If we are considerate, we plant the seeds for thoughtfulness in our future. If we appreciate the fact that this person has helped us to repay a karmic debt, and, consequently, react with kindness by deciding to have any anger stop here and now, then we have planted the seeds for understanding in our future.

When we start planting more seeds of consideration and selfless concern for the welfare of others, we will create good conditions in our future, as well as contribute to a better future for others. We can start doing this by realizing that as much as a person irritates us now, if we do not stop the escalation of anger, it will only get worse: The person who is irritating us now will keep doing so even more in the future. And the result will be two persons getting frustrated and angry, not just one—not just you. For his sake as well as our own, we need to stop this ugly exchange of anger.

Ideally, we will no longer worry about how we feel but be focused on how the other person feels, on how to free them from pain and unhappiness. At this point, we will be acting in accordance with our true nature. And the goodness that we create will be immeasurable, even enough to positively influence our current lifetime.

Deciding to Change

Liaofan's Four Lessons is the recorded account of Liaofan Yuan, a government official who lived in China almost five hundred years ago. As a young man, he was told exactly how his life would unfold, and for many years, everything happened exactly as he had been told. He became convinced that since a person's life was predestined, there was no need to try to do anything: What was supposed to happen would. As a result, he began to aimlessly coast through life.

After doing so for many years, he met an accomplished Zen master who explained to Liaofan how he could change what was destined to happen if he could correct his faults, change his selfish behavior, think only of benefiting others, and create goodness. Doing everything the master told him to do, Liaofan created so much goodness in his life that he was able to change his future.

Previously it was said that almost everything that happens in this lifetime is the result of our thoughts, speech, and physical behavior from past lifetimes. It is extremely difficult to change what is destined to happen in one's current lifetime, but that is what Liaofan did. He admitted to the master that one of his worst traits was his bad temper, which easily inflamed him with anger at the least provocation, and which made him critical, impatient, undisciplined. Yet with all of these as well as many other shortcomings, Liaofan developed new, positive ways of reacting to situations and other people. In this way, he completely changed his life.

He was destined to die at the age of fifty-three, but he lived until seventy-four. He was destined not to have children at a time when having sons to carry on the family name and bringing honor to one's ancestors was extremely important, but he and his wife had two sons. He was not destined to have a good job, but he retired as a respected government official.

Liaofan lived five centuries ago in China. How can we relate to a man who is so far removed from today's world? We can because what Liaofan learned was a universal truth that is not bound by time, geography, language, or cultural mores: We reap what we sow. He learned that all his problems—poverty, childlessness, his unfulfilling career—were all the results of what he had done previously. And his bad temper lay at the heart of his problems. So many things would set him off, not unlike today, when it seems that everything we encounter has the potential for angering us.

We, like Liaofan, can decide how we will react in the future to all those frustrating and infuriating situations we encounter. We might decide to control our tempers by promising ourselves that we will catch the anger before it gets out of hand, but this is very difficult to do for we will have to catch our anger before it erupts.

Another way to control anger is to understand causality: We become angry because of past thoughts, speech, and actions. Due to present thoughts, speech, and actions, if we do not modify our behavior now, we will suffer even more from our tempers in the future. This understanding will enable us to better overcome our anger.

The best way, however, is to have a change of heart. When we do so, we will have already begun to understand how hurtful and resentful criticism feels, and how uncomfortable and upsetting anger feels. We will also understand how hurt, resentful, and upset the other person feels. Eventually, empathizing with their pain and the pain of so many beings who suffer from the consequences of anger, our anger will dissolve and not even arise.

Overcoming our anger by watching our thoughts is very difficult: We have to be aware of each incident that irritates us so we can catch the anger before it erupts. Overcoming the anger by understanding causality is also difficult because we have to constantly remind ourselves of what is actually going on.

Overcoming and transforming anger and damaging, negative emotions is best accomplished by no longer having room for them in our hearts. Leave no place for thoughts of retaliation, ego, or defensiveness; only allow unselfish thoughts of helping others to grow.

We can do this in everything we do in our lives. The triggers for anger are encountered constantly: while driving, at work, at home or school, when we are with other people or alone. But everything depends on how we react. We can give in to the anger or we can realize that if somebody has said something unkind, instead of lashing back, we can overcome and transform the rising anger by choosing to react wisely and kindly. By doing this we can plant the seeds for all the good things that we want to happen in our lives.

Reflect within. Think about how we feel when we become angry. Contrast this with how we feel when we are calm and content. Think about the quiet state of serenity. Which do we prefer? The anger or the serenity? It is entirely up to us how we will feel in the future. It is entirely up to us what others around us will experience in the future. It is entirely up to us what our world and other people in this world, and other beings throughout the universe will experience. It all starts from within us. Serenity and joy start from deep within us, grow to include those around us, and then swell to include all those we meet. Ultimately, our serenity and joy will reach every being throughout the universe.

All this can happen if we just transform our anger and craving by illuminating our misunderstanding with the light of wisdom. Perhaps we were not taught, or if we were, we do not understand or do not believe. Whatever the cause, we do not truly understand. If we did, we would not behave as we do. We would not carelessly say things that hurt others. We would not ceaselessly be wanting more or constantly be giving in to anger. We would not continually be making the same mistakes over and over, lifetime after lifetime.

When we read or hear that our thoughts and actions will have consequences that we will have to bear in the future, many of us concur and nod in agreement. While we are reading or listening, we believe and accept. But, how long will we remember and how well will we understand after the book is closed or the speaker has ceased speaking?

We do not truly understand. We have been told, but we cannot remember, we cannot do, and we cannot change. So easily we fall back into those comfortable bad habits of desire and attachment, selfishness and anger. We try: We want to do what is good. We sincerely do not want to hurt another person, put ourselves first at the expense of others, or be consumed again by our anger. But as time passes, we slip back into forgetting.

Maybe, in this age of almost instant communication, we have become desensitized to wrong doings. What's a little bit more anger? A little bit more hate? A little bit more gossip? A little bit more falsehood? After all, everyone is doing it—stealing, coveting, lying. People argue, "Surely, the law of cause and effect does not apply to little indiscretions." But it does. It is a universal law, which means it applies 100 percent— not just 60 percent or 80 percent—of the time. In our desensitization, we conveniently rationalize that certain wrong actions are okay to do, that only certain wrong actions are truly wrong. So we devise our own little law of cause and effect. And we end up with knowing—but not fully understanding.

Our old habits blind us to remembering the principle of cause and effect. Maybe, if we can be reminded right away, or just before we do anything wrong, that a wrongful action is forthcoming, maybe we can stop our old bad habits. If only we can, just as when we hit our fingers (the cause) we feel pain (the effect), feel the consequences right away, maybe we will stop all our wrong doings. The fear of instant repercussions—in this case, instant throbbing pain in the finger—will surely stop further causes. Alas, most times we do not have such instant reminders. And so we slip back again and again, further and further, to knowing but not fully understanding.

A person who truly understands realizes that constantly wanting more is pointless, because we only need what we can reasonably use whether it is food, clothing, a place to live, or other necessities, and that we will not find happiness in wanting and obtaining "more." This wise person finds contentment in the appreciation of what we have.

A person who is aware knows that they feel much better when they are calm and undisturbed than when they are angry and agitated. This wise person understands the futility and danger of anger and chooses to let go of it.

The reality is that the wisdom is already within us as is contentment and serenity. Craving, anger, and unawareness are not our true essence, rather destructive habits that we have picked up. Although we have yet to become sincerely accomplished in all the practices of generosity and goodness, each of us can work to accomplish this goal.

By thinking of benefiting others instead of ourselves, by letting go of our anger instead of allowing it to grow and fester, by illuminating the darkness of unawareness with the clear light of understanding, we will transform ourselves from within, from our heart and mind. We can carry this determination with us. We can broaden that thought until it is our guiding thought. And then one day, we too will awaken to our perfect compassion, gentleness, and happiness.

CLIMATE CHANGE: WITH OUR THOUGHTS WE CREATE THE WORLD

Do no harm.
Do what is good.
Purify the mind.
If you cannot purify the mind,
then do no harm and do what is good.
If you cannot do what is good,
at the very least, do no harm.

Everything is manifested by the mind and altered by the consciousness. In other words, with our thoughts we create the world. As Buddhists, we learn that our greed results in floods. Angry thoughts result in fires, and ignorant thoughts are the cause of disasters involving wind. This is causality: every cause will have a result. As we continuously crave more power, more material goods and experiences, and we fail to obtain what we desire, the results—like natural disasters and environmental degradation—likewise intensify.

When we look around, consider what we see: prolonged drought; more frequent tornadoes; recording-breaking floods, hurricanes, and wildfires. These are the results of the three poisons of greed, anger, and ignorance. The terrible truth we are facing in the world today is that we are unable even to "Do no harm." We are poised at the brink of worldwide environmental collapse and have very likely already reached our "tipping point." This is the point at which we have gone too far and are no longer able to pull back from the plunge into the abyss. The question becomes "How deep is the abyss?" And then, "How did we get to this point?"

The more power and wealth politicians and companies want to have and the more comfort individuals seek to enjoy, the more we will harm the environment and every person, animal, and plant who struggle to exist in that environment. We are now experiencing the result: climate change. This now looming worldwide disaster has arisen from a very real cause—craving.

We consume more, thinking all the things we

crave will make us happy. But in reality we are depleting our nonrenewable resources and exhausting our planet. Toxic waste seeps into the earth and works its way into our rivers and oceans, contaminating everything it touches. Our imported goods and exotic foods are transported around the world on ships, planes, and trucks that spew toxic fumes and pump tons of carbon dioxide into the atmosphere. The rights of the poor to have clean water, arable land, and a safe place to raise their children are completely disregarded in the name of profit. As corporations become larger and larger, their preoccupation with the bottom lines makes them forget that those "purchasing units" are real people, struggling to live on this planet. One agribusiness fund manager gleefully said recently "Higher food prices are inevitable all over the world; we're in a sweet spot."

The more we buy and the less mindfully we live, the more we destroy what is natural and pure. In its place, we leave devastation. Tragically, we are committing unimaginable harm. Because of our greed and wish for control, we are coming precariously close to destroying our world as we know it.

Is there a way to stop this reckless behavior—a

way to behave responsibly and stop climate change? Is there still time? We do not know the answer to these questions. But we need to do everything within our power to try.

> Even if everyone else does not do what is right,
> I alone will.
> Even if everyone else is doing wrong,
> I alone will not.

The Result: Climate Change

Ice caps and glaciers melted. The world's most famous cities underwater. One-third of the planet turned to desert; the other two-thirds filled with people struggling for enough food and water to survive. Is this to be our future?

Our world is spiraling out of control and yet we still have leaders failing to take action on global warming. Newscasters and journalists report on how the stock market bounced back after some minor profit taking and what the latest tidbits from Hollywood are. People complain about the price of gasoline as they get back into their SUV and drive off, alone. Parents shake their heads and worry about how climate change will affect their children, then board the plane to go visit their children and grand-children because they love them.

On March 11, 2007, the *Sunday Times*, a major newspaper in the United Kingdom, detailed the earth-changing scenarios degree by degree that would likely occur in global warming. The article was an interview with Mark Lynas, the author of *Six De-grees: Our Future on a Hotter Planet* and referenced research by the Hadley Centre for Climate Change in the United Kingdom. Based on tens of thousands of pages of scientific research, *Six Degrees* provides a succinct analysis of what the world could look like after global warming:

> "At one degree of warming, the Arctic is ice-free for half the year, the South Atlantic—typically void of hurricanes—experiences coastal hurri-canes, and in the western U.S. severe droughts are plaguing residents.

Two Degrees of Warming: Polar bears struggle
to survive as glaciers increasingly melt away.
Glaciers in Greenland begin to disappear, while
coral reefs are vanishing.

Three Degrees of Warming: The Amazon rain
forest is drying out and El Niño's intense
weather pattern becomes the norm. Europe repeatedly experiences searing summer heat that
has rarely happened before.

Four Degrees of Warming: Oceans could rise,
taking over coastal cities. The disappearance of
glaciers may deprive many of fresh water.
Northern Canada's agriculture could boom and a
Scandinavian beach could be the next tourism
hotspot. A part of Antarctica could collapse,
causing water to rise even further.

Five Degrees of Warming: Uninhabitable zones
could spread, snow pack and aquifers feeding
big cities could dry up, and climate refugees
could run in the millions. Human civilization
could begin to break down with this drastic of

changes to the climate. The poor would likely suffer the most.

Six Degrees of Warming: The oceans could be marine wastelands, the deserts could march across continents, and natural disasters could become common events. The world's great cities could be flooded and abandoned. This could be 'the doomsday scenario.'"[1]

The Cause: Us

For the past 150 years, we were slowly drawn in by cheap, accessible energy. It became inevitable that the environmental costs of pollution and resource depletion, not borne by consumers, would fall on others. In time, as health care problems arose, these costs were borne by taxpayers who were not quite sure exactly where their tax dollars went. But as long as the system seemed to be working, few people were inclined to ask questions. Periodically a story would

---

[1] http://channel.nationalgeographic.com/channel/sixdegrees/

be on the news—the deplorable conditions miners labored under, increasing cancer rates, inequality issues—but people did not connect the dots. Most were engrossed with the commercials after the news and dreaming of what to buy next.

How did they get to this point? As consumers, after World War II, Americans became caught up in the government promoted dream of owning a house in the suburbs. There was seemingly endless land, government programs and loans for the soldiers returning home, and lots of cheap oil to power the dream. So Americans in record numbers began moving to the new suburbs. Dad drove into the city to work while Mom stayed home and looked after the children. It seemed idyllic.

But somewhere along the way, the dream of suburbia became complicated. People got caught up in the tragically mistaken idea that possessions and experiences would make them happy. The message they kept hearing was "more is better." Gradually, the houses became larger and families found themselves separated as grown children, now with their own dreams of an idyllic life, left home to work in other places.

Without the grandparents around to help care for the children, Mom needed to get a job to help pay for childcare. Dad found he needed to work longer hours to be able to afford all the good things they wanted for their children. Short on time, the parents turned to the new electronic help. Dishwashers, washing machines, and vacuum cleaners were soon deemed household necessities. The number of 'must have" electronic appliances increased as more products came to market.

But with planned obsolescence carefully calculated to increase corporate profits, the cars and all the other modern gadgetry needed to be frequently replaced. Since there was so much land and so many garbage dumps, the no longer wanted goods were simply thrown away. Plastic, polystyrene and other petroleum by-products that would take centuries to break down ended up at dumpsites. Toxins began to leach into the soil and groundwater. But it was okay because there was so much land.

As the list of modern conveniences grew, time-honored household skills were deemed old-fashioned and unnecessary in the modern world. The victory gardens that were a major source of food during the war gave way to lawns and flower beds. There was no need to cook anymore because there were TV dinners and prepared foods that could be quickly heated up by a Mom now very tired from working all day at the office or factory. There was no need to personally preserve foods anymore because there were lots of canned and frozen food in the supermarket.

Dad forgot the skills he had learned from his father because it was now easier to hire people to do what needed to be done. Plus, he had all those time-saving power tools and could buy ready-made items at the store. People, hooked on the electronic marvels to do their work, became increasingly dependent on all the cheap energy that powered their lifestyles.

Today, none of this has changed. We see people buying larger houses to store all the new electronic gear. The children, seeing Mom and Dad buying more, want their own televisions and computers just like all their friends have. Families might gather to eat dinner at the same time, but everyone heats up their own food in the microwave. After throwing away the microwavable containers, tossing the pizza carton in the trash, and putting the cutlery in the dishwasher, parents and children go to their own rooms. They then immerse themselves in their home entertainment centers or play games on their computers until it is time to go to sleep. Then in the morning, it's time to get up and begin all over again.

And so we have the American dream today, a dream that many people around the world want to have. But this is a dream gone terribly wrong.

Elephant in the Living Room

From deep within each person who begins to grasp the enormity of climate change and global warming, a profound sense of grief—and fear—begins to arise. Humanity's dream of prosperity is now becoming a nightmare. We are now learning what the future of our world will be like. And with this realization comes another: that six-degrees future has already begun. And it is even more horrific than we had feared.

Climate change has been called the "elephant in the living room." Think of it as a large, unruly guest who does whatever it wishes to do. But climate change is not the only elephant. Peaking oil, natural

gas, coal and uranium reserves are another four.
Then there is aquifer depletion and a human popula-
tion the size of which the earth cannot sustain. It
takes so much land and water to feed one human
and we have only a finite amount of these resources
in our world. Once we exceed that natural carrying
capacity, there is no longer enough food and water
for everyone.

Our current world situation is that we are at the
brink of an energy crisis that began with global oil
reserves peaking. The U.S. Energy Information Administration reported in 2007 that the peak occurred
in May 2005.[2] It is more difficult to gauge natural
gas reserves but it is generally accepted that they
have either also peaked or are close to doing so. Coal
and uranium are expected to peak around 2020 and
before 2050, respectively. Oil, natural gas, coal, uranium, and hydroelectric currently provide 93 percent
of the global energy supply. The remaining 7 percent
is mainly hydropower followed by biomass with a
fraction provided by renewables like solar and wind
power.

---

[2] U.S. Energy Information Administration, "Electric Power An-
nual for 2006 Report," released October 22, 2007

Peak resources means we have reached the point in time when the maximum production rate of the resource has been reached. Once past the peak, these natural resources will become increasingly difficult and costly to extract and process. As the prices rise, each of us will reach our personal peak, the point where our life is impacted negatively by the high cost brought about by ever-increasing competition for the remaining oil.

Also, we are moving closer to the point at which the extraction and production costs outweigh the energy obtained. We can see the logic in this with our food. It would make no sense to expend one hundred calories to eat food that will only provide ten calories of energy.

In addition to extraction, production and distribution costs, there are the hidden costs like pollution, aquifer depletion, soil degradation, and human health issues. These costs are not calculated in the price at the pump when we fill up our cars or at the store when we buy a box of imported chocolate encased in layers of plastic packaging. The costs are being borne by taxpayers and those who were forced off the land by governments and international conglomerates who are focused on profit not on climate change or the suffering of humans. These millions of economic refuges have no choice but to move into cities where they cannot find work or raise the subsistence crops that used to feed their families. The costs are borne by the children who must breathe polluted air, drink contaminated water, and live in squalid conditions—children who have no future for they will not be able to make a living or farm the land. Nor will they be taught by those who dispossessed them how to do provide for their own families in the future.

Understanding what *peak oil* means, what happens when we reach it?

The United States, the largest oil consumer, reached the peak of its domestic oil reserves in the 1970s. Now, when the United States is relying more heavily on imported oil, India and China are also becoming major oil importers. This is happening at the same time that domestic demand is increasing within the oil exporting countries. So countries like Venezuela and Saudi Arabia need to supply the increasing needs of their own citizens as well as their foreign customers.

As the gap between supply and demand increases, the price per barrel will continue to hit new highs. This is already happening. In the fall of 2004 a barrel of oil hit $50. Just three and a half years later, on March 12, 2008, oil hit $109.72. Already we are seeing people in the developed world having to decide whether to spend money on heating oil or on food, agonizing decisions those in the developing world have faced for years. What do people choose? They are choosing to buy heating oil because it takes longer for children to starve to death than it does or them to freeze to death.

Even if we have reached the maximum of global production, don't we still have a lot left? Surely we have plenty of time to come up with another solution to the increasing energy demands?

No, we do not have time because the ease and cost of extraction for the remaining reserves are very different from the already extracted oil both in quality and ease of extraction. Also, new solutions take a long time to develop. As reserves dwindle and become more difficult, and thus expensive, to extract, the quality grade of the oil also decreases as does the energy output per barrel. Higher oil prices reflect the additional production expense.

What about other energy-producing materials like tar sands? Tar sands are actually bituminous sands that are a natural mixture of sand, water, and bitumen. The largest reserves are in the oil sands in Canada and the tar sands in Venezuela, with smaller reserves in the United States, Russia, and the Middle East. These oil sands are not viscous like oil, thus they must be mined. This process takes much water and large amounts of energy to extract and process. This heavy crude oil is in turn expensive to process into gasoline, diesel fuel, and other products.

Currently, the government of Alberta, Canada has approved the extraction of the petroleum from the sands even though environmentalist say this complex process will create an environmental nightmare and thus hasten global climate change. The oil companies keep exploiting our fragile planet just to prolong the comfort of the wealthy who do not want to give up their personal comfort and consumptive lifestyles.

What about natural gas? The United States is now a net importer of natural gas. North American discoveries have been on a general decline since the early 1980s. Europe also hit the high of its natural

gas discoveries about the same time. Dr. Ali Samsam
Bakhtiari, former senior adviser to the National Ira-
nian Oil Company in Tehran, reported to the Austra-
lian Senate in 2006 that natural gas would peak
worldwide about 2008 or 2009. He also felt that
Russia had already peaked, which in turn directly
affected European imports.

Unlike oil, which can be easily transported in
tankers, gas has to be used onsite, or transported
through pipelines or in special tankers. So moving it
around is more problematic than oil.

What about coal? The World Coal Institute has
been saying for many years that there are enough
coal reserves to last for another 150 years. But the
Energy Watch Group, working with more recently
updated reserve numbers and factoring in the increasing rate of extraction due to increasing demand,
has calculated that the coal peak will occur somewhere between 2020 and 2030. China, the largest
consumer of coal is predicted to peak sooner.

Environmentally, coal is even more damaging than
oil or natural gas, as well as being far less efficient.
The Unites States has the world's largest coal reserves, but what has been extracted is the higher

grade anthracite coal, with a higher energy density than the lower grade lignite coal by a factor of five or six. Now, much of the remaining coal reserves are lignite not anthracite. So while coal production is increasing in the United States because of the lower quality of lignite, the energy output derived from this coal peaked around 1999. Consequently, the United States is now a net coal importer.

What about new technologies? Surely people are working on a solution. Won't something be invented that will provide for our future energy needs? Yes, we are now seeing developments in technologies like solar and wind but these currently provide just a fraction of one percent of our current energy supply. It will take time to increase both demand and supply. Richard Heinberg, author and peak oil educator, has said that it would take fifteen years for people to gradually replace their current petroleum-powered vehicles. So there is no quick transition even when we develop other technologies. Also, these technologies have their own environmental impact as solar voltaic arrays, windmills, and the other necessary equipment need to be produced and shipped. Then we face the "not in my backyard" syndrome. Everyone wants the new technology in place, but they do not want to have to look at it.

Also, for the size of what we are talking about, we need a national and even international energy distribution infrastructure. We do not have a magic fuel that we can simply plug into existing distribution systems. It will take national and regional government action to build a new energy grid. This will enable individuals and companies who produce more energy than they require to be shared with others.

Before a new technology can be produced and used, national governments need to do studies of the technology. Politicians need to poll their constituents, listen to special interest groups, and vote. If a bill is passed, funding needs to be found, and finally building needs to be done. Then, as we get closer to real production, we have a chicken-and-egg problem. Before companies will commit to participating in this new distribution system, they will want to see customers ready to use the new form of energy. But before customers install the commercial and residential systems to use the new technology, they will want to be sure the companies will supply the new form of energy. So which comes first—supply or demand?

The chicken or the egg?

As with any new technology, prices will be high to begin with. As production methods improve and more people purchase the item, the per unit cost will gradually be reduced and thus the new technology will become more affordable to a larger number of people. But even with lower costs, many people will want to wait for the old technology to wear out before replacing it with the new.

Hurdles to Overcome

We have to view the whole picture. Climate change, peak energy, aquifer depletion, soil degradation, and overpopulation—everything—is interrelated. In nature, if you tinker with one aspect, all the others are also impacted. We cannot ignore any of these other "elephants," for to do so will put at risk whatever good we might do regarding the others.

If we are going to have any positive influence on climate change and peak energy, we have to recognize these other eventual crises as well and incorporate solutions for all of them as we quickly adapt to our new reality. As the Buddha said, everything is interconnected; nothing exists on its own.

Cognitive dissonance

When faced with information that is drastically different from what one believes to be true, the tension has to be resolved through choosing either the familiar belief or the proposed new one. Most people will go with the belief they are familiar with.

When people, hearing about global warming and peak oil, look around and see that everything looks normal and feel that their lives are not that much affected, they tend to dismiss the new perspective. Yes, the price of gas and food has increased but surely that's just due to increased demand and corporate price gouging. Yes, the weather is unusual but that is normal. Yes, the ice is melting in Greenland, the Arctic, and in high-mountain glaciers but that could just be a temporary occurrence.

It is like putting a frog in an uncovered pot of water, placing the pot on the stove, and turning up the heat. Because the temperature increase is gradual, the frog keeps adapting to the increasing heat until it is too late, and the frog is boiled to death.

Economic Decline and Citizen Panic

When governments see their financial markets falling and imminent economic downturn, they will want to give in to corporate special interests and panicked voters. Shortsighted leaders will do as they have done for several decades: look for the quick fix. They will divert money from long-range plans to combat global warming and spend it on short-term economic injections of capital into the economy. But appeasing immediate demands to stop the pain will only insure even more terrible pain in the future.

Special Interest Groups

There are special interest groups who have funded organizations specifically set up to convince people that climate change is a hoax. Throughout history business has had close ties to those in power and today is no different. There are companies and individuals who are caught up in their craving for power and wealth. To onlookers, it seems amazing that these corporate giants and government officials seem to be completely disconnected from reality. Their children and grandchildren will have to live in the world they create. What on earth are they thinking? Whatever their reasons, these special interest groups make it difficult for people to learn the truth about global warming and deny them the time to make necessary changes.

What Can Governments Do?

Some things can only be done on a national or local government level. For example, to ensure equity and to slow down depletion, rationing systems for resources like gasoline, heating oil, and natural gas will need to be instituted. New energy policies and international treaties as well as large infrastructures to move energy more efficiently need to be done at the national and international level. New technologies need to be shared with developing countries. We also need national farm policies that will encourage backyard gardens and small farms. Large farms will need to grow more varied food in a sustainable way.

We need more flexible building codes and financial incentives for property owners and renters who install the efficient new-energy systems, improve the insulation in their homes and businesses, and incorporate ways to reduce their energy consumption.

Local communities need to focus on food availability and conservation measures. For example, in the United Kingdom and Australia, transition towns are planning to move away from reliance on existing energy sources into renewables. They are looking at how to support more efficient ways of manufacturing, provide more public transportation, use more efficient ways to heat and cool, and provide more secure food supplies that are much closer to home.

What Can Individuals Do?

If we live just for our own satisfaction and flawed perception of happiness, we will have little reason to make the sacrifices that we must make for humanity and all beings to allow them to survive in the future. Our only concern will be for "me" and "mine," meaning our immediate family and close friends. As resources become increasingly scarce, and thus increasingly costly, we will become even more self-centered and selfish. The more the fear sets in, the more self-centered will we become. Unless our depth of understanding is profound and deep-rooted, we will be overcome by our fear and we will fight to survive, at any cost.

Those who truly understand causality know the importance of every thought, word, and action. Our every decision will have consequences. Whenever we take more than our fair share, we are taking from another being. The suffering we cause others will come back to us.

We will pay the terrible cost for our indulgence.

As George Monbiot wrote in *Heat: How to Stop the Planet Burning*, "...the connection between cause and effect seems so improbable. By turning on the lights, filling the kettle, taking the children to school, driving to the shops, we are condemning people to death. We never choose to do this. We do not see ourselves as killers. We perform these acts without passion or intent."[3]

Behavior Change

Our parents worked very hard with the hope that

---

[3] George Monbiot, *Heat: How to Stop the Planet Burning*, (Cambridge, Mass., South End Press, 2007) 22.

our lives would be better than theirs. For many of us, our lives would appear better because we have more "stuff" and enjoy a broader range of experiences. But it is not enough for us. We are locked into behavior we seem unable to change. It is as if we are wearing blinders as we forge ahead determined to have one last final orgy of self-indulgence.

We have grown so used to our comforts that the thought of having to wash our clothes by hand, of walking more, of growing and then cooking—from scratch!—our own food seems like a return to the dark ages. Our expectations have far outrun the ability of our finite planet's resources to supply but we seem unwilling or unable to adjust to this reality.

The truth is that we have unthinkingly made many wasteful decisions regarding electricity production, transportation, and housing. George Monbiot calculated that the developed world needs to cut carbon emissions by 90 percent. Using the United Kingdom as an example, he shows how this is not impossible. Not knowing whether we will be able to make a difference by cutting back, we still need to try.

Changing Perceptions

"[M]uch of what is required...is simply coming to terms with the notion that a radical change in your way of life is not the same thing as the end of the world. I think many people tend to associate the two—we have always been wealthy and comfortable and lucky here in the west, and the loss of some or all of those things seems like a disaster of unimaginable proportions. But it doesn't have to be—that's a way of thinking we can choose to discard, recognizing that those who live less comfortable lives often value them equally."[4]

Relocalization

In the United States, food travels an average of 1500 miles to reach the consumer. On average, supermarkets keep only a three-day supply of food in stock. Small, locally owned stores have gone out of business, unable to compete with the Walmarts of the world. With globalization, manufacturing jobs have left the developed countries and gone overseas

---

[4] Anonymous comment, Casaubon's Book, "Hallowing the Descent," http://casaubonsbook.blogspot.com/2007/12/hallowing-descent.html, accessed December 27th, 2007

where labor is cheap, often because workers do not receive health or other benefits. In many countries, small farmers have gone out of business, unable to compete with government-subsidized agribusiness.

As energy prices continue to climb, the distribution of food over long distances will break down. There will be no guarantee that when we go to the supermarket there will be enough food for everyone. The solution is relocalization. Not only is it an economic solution, this is also a lifestyle solution. Agribusiness may be good for the companies but it is not good for consumers. Food transported 1500 miles loses much of its nutrition. But food that was picked yesterday and bought today at the local farmer's market is nutritious and so much better tasting. Organically grown and sustainably raised, it is good for the consumer, the farmer, and the environment.

Energy also needs to be provided on a local basis. Moving energy over long distances requires many resources. Peak energy means we will have much less access to the fuels we thought would last forever, or at least as long as we want them. But as resources dwindle, we will need to focus our lives much closer to home. Soon, our personal sphere of existence will be very small if we are to combat global warming by reducing carbon emissions. The fleeting concept of the global village will become a memory as our new priority becomes energy conservation. Long-range travel and cheap energy will soon be a thing of the past.

The upside is that we will build community as we get to know our neighbors, do business with local people, and grow much of our own food to provide food security. We only have to think back to the images of the people in New Orleans after hurricane Katrina to know that we need to depend on ourselves and our community.

Accepting Responsibility with Honor

In his book, *On Hallowing One's Diminishments*, the Quaker writer John Yungblut wrote,

> *"One might say with the Buddhists, that this [hallowing] is an important form of 'mindfulness' and try and cultivate the inner posture in which such consciousness can be relatively sustained.*

*Consulting the dictionary I find that for the
word 'hallowing' the following definitions are of-
fered: 'make holy or set apart for holy use, con-
secrate; to respect greatly; venerate.' It was a
new and most encouraging idea to me - that
one's diminishments could be 'made holy,' 'con-
secrated,' 'respected greatly,' even 'venerated.'*

*I saw that the first step for me in learning to 'hal-
low' the progressive diminishments in store for
me was deep-going acceptance. But the acceptance would have to be positive, not a negative
one, if it were to be a real hallowing. I must
learn to do something creative with it."*

We do not know whether we have enough time to
alter future events that have been put into motion by
so many people for so long. But we need to do everything we possibly can to try. We hear so often about
intention. Our intention in hallowing our diminishments of global warming and energy depletion is to
accept responsibility for what lies in our future. As
Sharon Astyk, a peak oil educator, wrote on her blog

"Casaubon's Book,"[5] "[W]e can come to recognize that sometimes, the point is not whether we can alter events, but how we face them. We can find meaning, even when we cannot change things, in our ability to shape the meaning of things - to do right, even when the right thing is not enough, to face even very hard times with courage and honor, even though it won't make the hard times go away to do so."

We can fight and rail against the things in life that feel so unfair. We can slip into pretending they do not exist. We can give up in despair. Or we can turn around to face that horror and work to understand why it is so terrifying. We can learn to face it with honor and thus, manage our fear.

What we are now facing are the consequences of our own past actions and decisions. Initially, we were unaware of what was happening, but now we know. We have been using up our natural resources and now they are running out. We have exported our style of living through movies, television, and other media. Now people around the world want to live like Americans do. But the reality is that Americans

---

[5] Ibid.

can no longer live as Americans have lived. The longer those of us who enjoy the privileges of wealth delay making the necessary changes, the harder it will be for all of us to face them later.

Previously, we did not think of what we were doing. Now we have come up against the reality of our actions. We can postpone what needs to be done or just make token efforts at making some changes. But if we fail to make the big changes—life-altering changes—our children and grandchildren will be forced to inhabit a world terribly different from the one we have been so privileged to enjoy.

If we can hallow our diminishments, we will find some benefits—a stronger sense of community and family, the knowledge that we tried to do the right thing when we realized that we had done some of the worst.

The Buddha taught about impermanence, how everything is continuously changing. Each of us has changed from who we were just a minute ago. Some cells have died, others have replaced them. These are minor changes, not even noticeable. We still function as we did a minute ago even though we have changed.

But climate change? No more cheap oil and, eventually, no oil at any price? Not enough natural gas? Not enough water? These are terrifying. When we come face-to-face with the changes that we feel are overwhelming and more than we can handle, we initially react from our fear. We say it cannot possibly be true. We say those who suffer from inadequate resources and natural disasters suffer due to their karma. Or we look for ways to disprove what people are saying. Or we choose to do nothing as we abruptly shut the door in the messenger's face.

As a commenter wrote on Astyk's blog "I think cognitive dissonance has much to do with our collective denial of responsibility. We're unwilling to sacrifice a standard of living that cannot be sustained without exploiting others. So instead of changing, we find ways to minimize the truth and blame our victims for their troubles. People shut out clear, rational arguments that don't fit with their world view and self-concept. Our self-esteem is totally wrapped up with consumption. We have been told since we were children that having lots of stuff is what makes us 'winners' in life. We don't want to give anything up— it would be giving up a part of ourselves that we've worked hard to create and nourish. That's why people get so completely defensive and pissed off when you bring up this subject—you're messing with their self-esteem and sense of self-worth. I'm not just pointing the finger at others. I also plead guilty."[6]

So there is a lot going on in people's reactions to words like global warming and resource depletion. The reactions revolve around change. We usually do not like it. The Buddha taught that change permeates life. That just as our minds are continuously changing, phenomena are also continuously changing. Everything is manifested by the mind and altered by the consciousness and thus, with our thoughts we change the world. And yet, we still believe that we can keep living as we have been doing. We doubt, debate, and deny. But doubting, debating, and denying will not help us fix this new, frightening world of ours.

Nor will what we have been told to do for the past sixty years—go shopping—solve this problem. We believe buying things we will make us happy. But studies show people were happier in the 1950s. Yes

---

[6] Ibid.

they had less—less stuff. But they had time for their children, they worked fewer hours, and they felt more secure. It was safe for children to walk to school. People could leave their doors unlocked. But then, we were told to buy more, that by doing so we would be really happy.

We have seen the results of looking for happiness in consuming. It does not work. This is hardly news since the Buddha taught over 2500 years ago that happiness does not lie in new things or experiences. Happiness is to be found within ourselves, it lies in what we tell ourselves. Happiness is a mental state, not a physical state.

The earlier we realize happiness does not lie in consumption, the earlier we will realize we cannot consume ourselves out of what is now happening. It is going to take more than changing light bulbs and carrying reusable cloth shopping bags. These are of course an excellent start, but that is all—a beginning.

We need to make changes in our lives, in every aspect of our lives. What we tell ourselves about those changes will determine how we feel. We can make the changes, or we can doubt, debate, and deny. We can complain, or we can hallow those changes by honoring them and accept responsibility for what we have done. We can learn to live with the changes, understanding that doing so is, as Astyk says, "not an unjust cruelty, but simply what is asked of us, our share of the burden."

Peak oil, water depletion, and climate change are some of the most destructive conditions that could happen to society and this planet we live on. But they are what we have created. Very simply, they are cause and effect. Initially, we acted out of ignorance. At some level, we knew there was only so much oil and natural gas, but we figured some clever person would come along and fix things for us. They would find a new form of energy or invent a better technology. It was not anything we needed to be concerned about.

Ignorance is one of the three poisons the Buddha so often warned about. The other two poisons? Greed and anger. Indeed, with our thoughts we create the world. So not only from the everyday standpoint, but from the karmic standpoint, we have created and are currently creating the world we will be living in. The environmental changes we are now beginning to experience are not an unjust punishment inflicted on us. We have recklessly exploited our planet and now we will be paying for our actions. How will we justify what we have done when our children and grandchildren inherit the world from us? When they realize how we have lived, they will wonder what we were thinking. Why did we not change when we learned of the immense harm we were doing? How could we have cared so little? For the world's children? For our own?

It is up to us to face our diminishments now, when we still have a choice. To do so when we are forced to would be irresponsible, and largely futile. Now at least, we still have some time to change the way we do things.

And this is where the hallowing comes in, for there are benefits to be had if we just recognize and honor them. We will have more time with family and neighbors, benefit from healthier lifestyles, learn more about ourselves, and maybe, just maybe, help save the future for our children and our planet.

Life in forty, twenty, even ten years will be very different from what it is now. We need to come together and learn what to do, both on a community level and as responsible individuals. We live in a uni-

verse that adheres to the law of cause and consequence. The consequences are not within our control. But our current karmas, our current actions, are.
Honoring and respecting resource depletion and climate change are within our control and ability.

We need to do everything within our power to hallow these diminishments, for they are ours.

Ways to Reach Us

E-mail: amitabha-publications@runbox.com
www.chinkung.org   www.amtbweb.org

Australia [61]

Amitabha Buddhist Association of NSW,Inc.
Tel: 2-9643-7588   Fax: 2-9643-7599

Amitabha Buddhist Association of Perth
Tel: 8-9306-8120   Fax: 8-9306-8366

Amitabha Buddhist Association of QLD
Tel: 7-3273-1693   Fax: 7-3272-0677
E-mail: amtb@amtb-qld.org.au

Amitabha Buddhist Retreat Centre
Tel: 7-4171-0421   Fax: 7-4171-0413
E-mail: amitabhacentre@hotmail.com

Pure Land Learning Center of the NT
Tel: 8-8927-4988   Fax :8-8981-3516
E-mail: amitabhacentre@hotmail.com

Pure Land Learning Center of Victoria
Tel: 3-9891-7093   Fax: 3-9891-7093
E-mail: purelandvic@yahoo.com

Pure Land Learning College (Toowoomba)
Tel: 7-4637-8765   Fax: 7-4637-8764
Web: www.amtb-aus.org
E-mail: purelandcollege@iinet.net.au

Canada [1]

Amitabha Buddhist Association of Ottawa
Tel: 613-723-9683   Fax: 613-723-6316
Web: www.amtb-ottawa.ca
E-mail: info@amtb-ottawa.ca

Amitabha (Six Harmony) Buddhist Org.
Tel: 416-265-9838   Fax: 905-947-1870
E-mail: amtb6hcan@yahoo.ca

Amitabha Buddhist Association of Montreal
Tel: 514-257-1770   Fax: 514-525-6846
E-mail: amtbmontreal@gmail.com

The Amitabha Buddhist Society of Toronto
Tel: 416-293-0024   Fax: 416-292-6061

United Kingdom [44]

Buddhist Education Foundation (UK)
Tel: 171-586.6923   Fax: 171-7948594
Web: www.buddhisteduation.co.uk

Hong Kong [852]

Hong Kong Buddhist Education Foundation
Tel: 2314-7099   Fax: 2314-1929
Web: www.budaedu.org.hk
E-mail: amtbhkl@budaedu.org.hk

Malaysia [60]

Amitabha Buddhist Society(Malaysia)
Tel: 3-4041-4101   Fax: 3-4041-2172
Web: www.amtb-m.org.my
E-mail: amtbmy@pd.jaring.my

Singapore [65]

Amitabha Buddhist Society(Singapore)
Tel: 6744-7444   Fax: 6744-4774
Web: www.amtb.org.sg

Singapore Buddhist Lodge
Tel: 6737-2630   Fax: 6737-0877
Web: www.amtb.org.sg

Spain [34]

Amitabha Buddhist Society(Spain)
Tel: 1-522-3603   Fax: 1-522-7151

Taiwan [886]

The Corporation Republic of Hwa Dzan Society
Tel: 2-2754-7178   Fax: 2-2754-7262
Web: www.amtb.org.tw
www.chinkung.org
E-mail: hwadzan@amtb.org.tw

Kaohsiung Pureland Society
Tel: 7-521-9988   Fax: 7-521-1895
E-mail: amtb@xuite.net

Thailand [662]

Amitabha Buddhist Society
Tel: 719-5206   Fax: 719-4356

United States of America [1]

Amida Society
Tel: 626-286-5700   Fax: 626-286-7988
Web: www.amtb-la.org
E-mail: amida@amtb-la.org

Amita Buddhism Society-Boston
Tel/Fax: 508-580-4349
Web: www.amtb-ma.org
E-mail: amtb_boston@yahoo.com

Amitabha Buddhist Association of State Washington
Tel: 425-251-6822   Fax: 425-656-9789

Amitabha Buddhist Library in Chicago
Tel: 630-416-9422   Fax: 630-416-6175
Web: amitabhalibrary.org
E-mail: info@amitabhalibrary.org

Amitabha Buddhist Society of Hawaii
Tel: 808-523-8909   Fax: 808-523-8909

Amitabha Buddhist Society of Houston
Tel: 713-339-1864   Fax: 713-339-2242

Amitabha Buddhist Society of Michigan
Tel: 734-995-5132   Fax: 734-995-5132

Amitabha Buddhist Society of New Jersey , Inc.
Tel: 856-751-7966   Fax: 856-751-2269
E-mail: njbuddha@comcast.net

Amitabha Buddhist Society of NY , Inc.
Tel: 718-961-7299   Fax: 718-961-8039
E-mail: amitabha_ny@yahoo.com.tw

Amitabha Buddhist Society of Seattle
Tel: 206-624-9378

Amitabha Buddhist Society of Philadelphia
Tel: 856-424-2516   Fax: 856-489-8528
Website:www.amtb.org
E-mail: amtbphila@hotmail.com

Amitabha Buddhist Society of USA
Tel: 408-736-3386   Fax: 408-736-3389
Website:www.amtb-usa.org
E-mail: info@amtb-usa.org

Amitabha Educational Center(Hawaii)
Tel: 808-262-5279   Fax: 808-262-4989

Amitabha Society of Las Vegas
Tel: 707-252-3042   Fax: 707-871-3542

Atlanta Amitabha Buddhist Society
Tel: 770-923-8955   Fax: 770-925-0618
E-mail: mietoville@bellsouth.net

Dallas Buddhist Association
Tel: 972-234-4401   Fax: 972-234-8342
Web: www.amtb-dba.org
E-mail: amtbdba@yahoo.com

May the merits and virtues
accrued from this work
adorn the Buddha's Pure Land,
repay the Four Kindnesses above,
and relieve the sufferings of those
in the Three Paths below.

May those who see or hear of this
bring forth the Bodhi mind,
and at the end of this life,
be born together
in the Land of Ultimate **Bliss**.

DEDICATION OF MERIT

*May the merit and Virtue accrued from this work
adorn Amitabha Buddha's Pure Land,
Repay the four great kindnesses above, and
relieve the suffering of those on the three paths below.*

*May those who see or hear of these efforts generate
Bodhi-mind, spend their lives devoted to the
Buddha Dharma, and finally be reborn together
in the Land of Ultimate Bliss.
Homepage to Amita Buddha !*

Venerable Wuling

Everything
We Do
Matters

✠ Donator : Amida Society

✠ Address : 5918 Cloverly Ave, Temple
City, CA. 91780 U.S.A.

✠ Web Site : www.amtb-la.org

✠ TEL : (626)286-5700 : 282-3700

✠ FAX : (626)286-7988

✠ Design : Kaohsiung Pureland Society

✠ Printer : White Stone Publisher (07)553-0299

Printing October 2010 *1000 copies
Made in Taiwan